# You Can't Do It Naked

*From Exposed to Fully Clothed in the Armor of God*

KIM M. SNYDER, MS, LPC

# REVIEWS

I love the conviction and confidence in Kim's voice, the wisdom from someone who's been through spiritual battles and knows how to fight them. She uses vivid examples from the scriptures, and tells the stories "Snyder-style," in her own unique way. *You Can't Do it Naked* has inspired me and motivated me to be a better Christian, and to more effectively use the tools God has given us to defeat our enemy. This book is a must-read for anyone who feels besieged by the struggles we all face in life.

**—Elayne Wells Harmer, J.D., Senior Editor for RMS Productions**

Have you ever read scripture or heard a sermon about the Armor of God? Many times, we hear God's word and do not have clear understanding of the message. Other times we may understand His word, but are not certain how it applies to our lives. In *You Can't Do It Naked*, Kim Snyder beautifully shares how and why we all need to put on the full Armor of God. With wisdom and authenticity, Kim shares openly the difficulties we encounter when we "go naked"—without God's Armor—as we journey through life.

Kim explains how our enemy, Satan, tries to keep us from living life to the fullest. She doesn't let this truth discourage us, but rather boldly encourages and empowers us to defeat the enemy by putting on the full armor of God. *You Can't Do It Naked* describes each part of the Armor: how to put it on, how it protects us, and how it helps us experience "Abundant Life." This is a must read! Thank you, Kim, for your gift in sharing God's Truth in love, humor, and wisdom. Wonderfully written.

**—Shelley Wine, M.A.L.L.P., Family Counselor**

In a word: powerful! Kim gives practical examples of day-to-day challenges and struggles in life, and shows us how to deal with them. She has not only shown us God's tools we can use to fight our battles, but she teaches how we can find the solutions with God's help. *You Can't Do it Naked* opened my eyes and my heart to things I didn't want to see, hear, or feel. But I am so happy I did! This book is meant to be a resource throughout your life. Keep it at your fingertips, and read it over and over. Just like God, it will be right there for you when you need strength.

**—Cindy Clark, CC Transformational Coaching, Health/ Wellness and Personal Coaching**

# DEDICATION

This book is dedicated to all warriors who have ever fought spiritual and emotional battles—especially those who are fighting them today.

*You do not need to fight in this battle. Stand firm, hold your position, and see the salvation of the Lord on your behalf...*
2 Chron. 20:17 (ESV)

# ACKNOWLEDGMENTS

**God**—I can't imagine my life without you in it. You repeatedly prove your love for me, in good times and especially in bad. I continually learn more about you as I face events and trials, and with every turn, you are faithful in all your promises. May I continue to be a vessel for you!

**Tim**—Thank you for coming into my life and being my source of laughter and love. I could not have progressed in my life's dreams and desires if you had not stepped in to be Mr. Mom, Taxi Driver, Chef, Maid, and a host of other roles too numerous to mention. You have flawlessly stood by my side in all my serious and crazy endeavors. I am truly blessed by you, my love. SHMILY— "Yes, I do!"

**Kayla, Corey, and Amelia**—The moment I became a mom, my life changed—even more so when I became a grandmother. Through mothering you, I have been blessed to understand in a very real way how much God loves his children. There are no words that could adequately define my deep love for you. You are a blessing to me in every way!

**Katie, Becky, and (soon to be) Grayson**—My life is enriched by every adventure we have experienced together. You have done more to help develop and strengthen my character than you could possibly know. Blended families are tough, but we rode out the storms and have come out on the other side very blessed! I love you.

**Sherry, Angie, Shelley, and Chris**—You are my lifetime friends, confidants, and spiritual warriors. Each of you plays a very unique and intricate role in my life; every one of you knows a separate, intimate piece of who I am. I am richly blessed to have you by my side. Having each of you—at a moment's notice—willing to laugh, pray, cry, vent, and just be a little crazy together means more than you know. These moments of release keep me sane!

# TABLE OF CONTENTS

# THE PURPOSE OF THIS BOOK

We live in a fallen world. All of us have fallen away from God's grace into sin, and the subsequent struggles we face can feel completely unbearable. These battles—doubt, diminished self-worth, depression, anxiety, temptations, and addictions are only a few—leave us feeling helpless and hopeless, as though we've been defeated in war.

There is an adversarial power at work that fights against us and wants us to fail. We are riddled with weaknesses and addictions; we often lack the strength to do the right thing. This dark power wants us to believe the lies that insist "you just can't do it, you can't get over it, you can't overcome it." The adversary has flooded our lives with so many lies, it's hard to know what truth really is—until now. This book will give you the tools you need to discern reality from deception.

Satan, our adversary, has turned everything upside down. When we are broken by shame and guilt, our emotional and spiritual vulnerability exposes us to Satan. Without the protection of the Armor of God, we are left defenseless against the enemy's lies. Naked, we feel every sting and believe every lie, and slowly those deceptions become the twisted "truth" in which we unknowingly begin to walk.

If you are reading this book, take hope—because all is about to change! Despite sin and weakness, none of us needs to remain vulnerable to Satan's attack. We have been given a shield of protection; we have access to the amazing "Armor of God." *You Can't Do It Naked* will help you recognize why and how Satan is attacking us, and who we can become when we look to Christ for help. This book is about learning to move from being emotionally and spiritually vulnerable to being fully armored. *You Can't Do It Naked* will shift your focus from physical weakness to spiritual strength, and will help you walk by faith, not by sight.

Being fully armored allows you to show up and stand firm while the Lord fights your battles.

This book is for all those who are sick and tired of being emotionally and spiritually sick and tired; those who have exhausted themselves trying to fight battles they can't seem to win. This book is for those who have never heard of the Armor of God—or for those who have, but are unsure how to get it and how to wear it.

This book is not a physical step-by-step lesson plan for you to follow, nor will it give you a checklist of physical things to do to help you navigate through your battles. The root of our struggles is spiritual. Like most people, you have probably attempted every kind of physical remedy, checklist, or journal to help you. Reading this book indicates that you are done fighting those battles on your own, and you're ready to become a mighty warrior with God helping you suit up.

I hope this book will change your way of viewing and thinking about your problems. You believe you are fighting the things you "see"—physical weaknesses, sins, or addictions—but you're not. The battle is spiritual—and so are the weapons. This book will help you identify not just what a spiritual battle is, but who your adversary is, and where the battle can be fought and won. When you have finished this book, you will be able to identify the value of the Armor of God and know how these spiritual pieces can be internally worn.

I am passionate about this subject for several reasons. I am a licensed Christian counselor, and I see clients every day who are completely broken down by the heart-wrenching struggles and challenges they face. But the power of the Armor of God is like nothing I have ever witnessed. I've seen clients who had struggled with debilitating addictions and weaknesses for years, yet once they learned to use God in their battles, they could finally break the chains and set themselves free. I've seen the astonishing effects that wearing the Armor of God can have on suicidal clients—renewing their hope and restoring the value of their lives.

On a more personal note, I recently lost my sister to cancer. She had the greatest giving heart, yet she was spiritually "naked": without God at the center of her life, she was emotionally vulnerable to the attacks of Satan. His lies destroyed the quality of her life and kept her from reaching her full potential. She wasn't unique in that sense; Satan has deceived us all by telling us we can't change, we can't overcome.

I struggled with acceptance most of my life. You'll hear my story inside this book, and you'll see how putting on the Armor of God changed my life. It can change yours, too. I invite you to take this journey with me. The Armor of God will enable you to see things as they really are, and it will empower you to see the truth about who and what you are really fighting. By learning to wear the Armor of God, you too can transform your nakedness into a fully dressed spiritual warrior.

May God bless you in your transformation and journey to freedom.

# INTRODUCTION

When you hear the word "naked," what does it make you think of? Does your mind see exposed flesh, or do you feel the discomfort of being naked? Imagine yourself naked standing on a street corner, or maybe being naked getting up on stage to speak to a crowd of thousands! Or maybe standing naked on a battlefield where arrows are flying everywhere, and there you are without a way to shield yourself, with no armor to withstand the blows of the battle.

"Being naked" is a metaphor for being emotionally and spiritually vulnerable. "Being naked" means being exposed to our adversary in a way that leaves us emotionally unprotected, stripped of anything and everything that can shield us from his attacks, leaving us unable to extinguish the fiery arrows he relentlessly throws at us.

What are his fiery arrows? The emotional lies he tells us that knock us off our game and cause us to doubt ourselves and others. These arrows can leave their mark on you in ways you never expected. Up until now, you've been battling the "symptoms" of being attacked, while the real issue, the "root," has gone unexamined.

I am a Christian Licensed Professional Counselor. I've seen hundreds—perhaps thousands—of clients who are so focused on the symptoms of their struggles that they cannot see who and what they are truly fighting.

In my private counseling practice, I have seen many clients move from being completely naked (emotionally vulnerable)—feeling powerless over their lives and weighed down by their beliefs—to becoming a fully Armored Warrior, empowered and strengthened by their understanding of how to fight emotional wars.

If you've ever doubted your own worth, or if you've suffered from anxiety or depression, then you are no stranger to emotional wars. If you feel like the arguments you're having with your spouse/mate seem to get totally out of control, then you too are fighting an emotional war.

*You Can't Do It Naked* will help you learn how to cover yourself with the true protection of our Lord. It will help you learn how to become keenly aware of the schemes, tricks, and strategies of the devil. You've heard the saying "the battle belongs to the Lord," but few know how to truly prepare for that battle so that the Lord is doing the fighting—not you.

*You Can't Do It Naked* will help you become fully armored and dressed for battle. You will become a mighty warrior, courageously standing firm on the battlefields of emotional and spiritual wars. You will stand firm with confidence and watch as our Lord and Savior successfully fights your battles.

You were designed to be a skillful warrior, and God has not left you to fight that battle unprepared, unprotected, or alone. I am excited to begin this transformation process with you. I can help you transform yourself into a Mighty Warrior—a warrior who knows the strategies of his enemy, who is fully dressed and prepared for battle.

# 1

## IN THE BEGINNING

*So God created man in his own image, in the image of God he created him; male and female he created them. . .. And God saw everything that he had made, and behold, it was very good...*

*Gen. 1:27, 31*

We all have a beginning. I don't mean the beginning of life—I mean the beginning of our struggles, when we first began to believe the lies of the adversary. We can't really remember how it started or when we learned a technique for coping with struggles, but we did. Of course, that isn't saying we learned an effective way. Our very first exposure to self-worth came from our holding or nurturing environment: parents, grandparents, siblings, extended family, peers, and teachers.

Now, I'm not trying to throw parents under the bus (I'm a parent of four myself), but our personalities and emotional triggers started when we were very young. As much as it hurts us to hear it, a child's first feelings of self-worth or self-hate come from what our parents say to and about us.

As a counselor, I have repeatedly observed that a coping mechanism that works for a child—to address real or perceived conflict—rarely works when the child becomes an adult. Most of us don't have any resources to draw from other than our childhood experiences. We usually keep doing the same thing over and over, expecting a different result. As you've probably heard, that's the definition of insanity—but it's too harsh for most of us. I like this saying better: "Our thought process which gets us into trouble can't be the same thought process to get us out of it." In other words, we need a different plan to combat emotional warfare.

The problem is, we don't easily discard ineffective behaviors. In fact, in the heat of the moment, we usually respond in the way we always have. That old behavior is what we know, even if what we know is ineffective, abusive, and downright hurtful. Without living and thinking with intent, we become the exact thing we wanted to *not* become.

Here are some examples. Perhaps you had a parent who was addicted to drugs or alcohol. A person under the influence is very different when sober or straight, and the inconsistency probably made you feel very anxious as a child. Maybe your parents got divorced and you missed the one you saw infrequently, or not at all. Maybe the divorce wars left you feeling fearful and insecure, or like you needed to choose between parents.

Perhaps you had a critical parent. His or her motive and intent may have been to motivate you to be better, yet how they attempted to motivate might have left you feeling hurt, manipulated, or incapable.

Does any of that sound familiar? If you're like me, you too have a story, and these stories continue to play out into adulthood. The choices we make today are directly related to how we have responded to our experiences since childhood—or, more importantly, how we have accepted the lies we believed during these experiences (you're a failure, you have no worth, bad things are your fault, etc.). Natural temperament plays a big part in how we respond to these events. Our choices do too, of course, but many of us don't choose to react in a mindful way. We just react.

My Story
Speaking of temperament, let me tell you about mine. As a child, I was quiet and reserved; I was a lurker, not saying much. I had a speech impediment as a young girl, and couldn't say my Rs.

My dad belonged to the Spokesman's Club at our church. One day, he brought home a tongue twister he wanted me to practice. He was sure that with time and practice, I would overcome the weakness in the muscle in my tongue (that's how specialists described my problem). I was excited to try it. The card read:

*Around the rugged rock, the ragged rascal ran.*

But that's not at all how it sounded when I said it:

*Awound the wugged wock, the wagged wascal wan.*

Strange, just writing that sentence sends me right back to being a young Elmer Fudd. Yes, I'm keenly aware of what teasing feels like.

Consequently, I didn't talk much. Over time, I did manage to strengthen that muscle in my tongue, but it never went away completely. You'll still hear it when I get tired, or if I have a couple of drinks, or when I put together consecutive words with a W and an R (i.e., white rabbit).

I had an older sister who was nothing like me in many aspects. Our temperaments were polar opposites: Terrie was bold and outgoing, willing to speak up against anything she didn't agree with, while I was restrained and introverted.

We responded to life's situations in opposite ways as well. We grew up in a fairly strict home—our parents have long since mellowed out, but when we were younger, we struggled to find that comfortable place where we could relax and just be. We needed a place from judgment, where we didn't have to walk on eggshells, where we could make mistakes and grow from them, instead of being punished. Temperament plays a big part in how you respond to things, and my sister and I were textbook examples. You either try to find that comfortable place, or you believe the lie that you won't find it and you stop trying. Me? I kept trying to attain some level of feeling whole and accepted. I believed the lie that I just needed to do one more thing. Terrie? She believed the lie that no matter what she did, she wouldn't get it right. Strange how early those lies begin to creep into your head. I was never aware that I was naked and unprotected in front of the adversary—nor was my sister.

Now, Terrie was very smart—probably too smart for her own good—but she had a rebellious streak. She wasn't rebellious for the sake of being rebellious, although from the outside perhaps it might have seemed so. No, she was rebellious against what she felt was disrespect—towards her, and towards others.

That's part of my beginning. I'm sure it started much earlier than that, but it's the beginning of my memories. As you go further into this book, I'll reveal something else about myself—the lie that led me to believe I was flawed and unaccepted.

### Adam and Eve's Beginning

Our first parents, "in the beginning," started in the garden:

*And the man and his wife were both naked and were not ashamed.*

Gen. 2:25

Naked in the garden and shameless—the way it was meant to be. They were vulnerable and naked to the Lord.

What pure emotional freedom this represents! But what happened? We all know the story: Adam and Eve engaged in a cunning conversation with the serpent, Satan, and then they ate the fruit from the Tree of Knowledge of good and evil. Everything we know about the human race changed in that moment, right?

Every time I heard that story as a kid, my focus was always on the fruit. I wondered what kind of fruit tree it was. (*Squirrel!* I know—stay focused on the story, Kim!) The poor apple got a bad rap— the story was not about the apple.

In fact, the story never even tells you what fruit it really was. As I got older, my focus changed to something else. I re-read that story and began focusing on something other than the fruit.

*The Lord God took the man and put him in the garden of Eden to work it and keep it. And the Lord God commanded the man saying, "You may surely eat of every tree of the garden, but of the tree of knowledge of good and evil you shall not eat, for in the day that you eat of it you shall surely die."*

Gen. 2:15-17

It isn't until verse 18 that we read it wasn't good for Adam to be alone! THERE IT IS! God had the conversation with Adam about not eating of the Tree of Knowledge. Of course! I wanted to blame *Adam* for Eve eating the fruit. I wanted to blame Adam for poor communication skills and not being clear when he told his wife not to eat of it.

Anyone married to a spouse with poor communication skills? That must be what happened! I'm not alone in this blaming thing, either; Adam and Eve did it as well. I'll get to that in a moment.

The beginning of Genesis 3 is the account of the conversation with Satan and Eve and how Eve "believed the lie"—she was convinced the tree was good for her. She then gave the fruit to Adam, and he ate of it.

Here is where their "nakedness" began. Remember, back in Genesis 2:25 we are told they were naked but not ashamed (in front of God). But in the next chapter we read,

*Then the eyes of both were opened, and they knew that they were naked . . .*

Gen. 3:7

Immediately after they ate the fruit, they felt naked. Being "physically" naked is not what this is all about, but I'll get to that in a moment.

Now, back to the blaming. This is how we have learned to handle our "stuff." Right from the very beginning, we humans have learned to blame and point the finger at someone else for why we do what we do.

In the garden, God looks for Adam and Eve. They had a desire to cover themselves, so they shielded themselves with fig leaves and hid. *"Where are you?"* God asks. Adam is the first to respond to God, but look what he says:

> *"The woman whom you gave to be with me, she gave me fruit of the tree, and I ate."*

Gen. 3:12

Seriously? Bone of your bone, flesh of your flesh, and you throw her under the bus, Adam? But he keeps going with the blame theme and starts the finger-pointing, and it's a double doozer! He then blames God because He gave him the woman and it was she who gave him the fruit! Wow, that is brassy, Adam! But, like almost every other human in existence, myself included, no one likes the underside view of a bus. The blame game doesn't stop with Adam.

God then turns to Eve and fingers continue to fly when she tells God:

> *"…The serpent deceived me, and I ate."*

Gen. 3:13

Ah, here it is: the first in a long line of "the devil made me do it" excuses!

As a young woman rereading this story once again, I realized I was reacting like Adam and Eve. I was looking for someone to blame, and I first picked Adam as the culprit for poorly communicating God's directives to his wife.

I was just like them; I was pointing my finger at everything and everyone for why the things in my life weren't going well. It was my parents; it was my ex-husband; it was everyone but me. I too wanted to use the-devil-made-me-do-it excuse for why I was on a detour in my life. I was naked and ashamed and looking for whatever I could use to cover myself.

I'm so glad God continues to help me grow and refocus (and so is my husband, Tim!). Here is where God has me refocusing at this point in my life. I want to draw your attention away from the tree, away from the blaming of others, toward Adam and Eve's nakedness and their desire to be covered.

God, in His divine wisdom, created our need to be covered, to be shielded. Humans instinctively pick something physical to cover themselves. God picks something else. But, right out of the gate, we can't understand the concept of spiritual. No, we need a physical representation of what "spiritual" actually means. The Bible is written with that understanding—that's how we learn of the spiritual meaning. The story of Adam and Eve's clothes is no exception.

God replaced their fig leaves with the skins of animals. This is future-focused; this is a prophesy. Something innocent needed to die to cover them. Isn't this what the death of Jesus Christ does for us?

This is what the story in the Garden of Eden points to—the Savior. We must be covered, but what do we cover ourselves with? With the Armor of God.

*You Can't Do It Naked* is about our journey of discovery to literally being covered by God. Just as Eve was vulnerable to the master of all lies—the serpent, the devil—so too are we. God did not leave us ill-equipped to handle the battles we will most assuredly face in our lives.

God knows the devil is after us.

> *Put on the whole armor of God, that you may be able to stand against the schemes of the devil. . . . Therefore, take up the whole armor of God, that you may be able to withstand in the evil day, and having done all, to stand firm.*

Eph. 6:11, 13

You can't do it naked; you must ARMOR UP.

### Your Beginning

Where does your beginning start? I'm talking about the beginning of your troubles. I'm talking about the beginning where you first remember you began to believe the lies—the lie of doubt, the lie of low self-worth, the lie of believing you have little value to offer the world, or maybe the lie that you are unlovable or not worthy of love. Or worse yet, you believe the lie that you deserved it—that whatever bad thing happened to you, it was your fault.

These lies usually start when you're young. Even the best-intentioned parent can unknowingly cast some of these lies upon us. They might be in the form of wanting us to get better grades or doing better on the sports team. Innocent as their motives might appear, the way they speak can leave us feeling like we don't measure up to their standards.

The lies become entangled with truth, and over time it's difficult to discern their differences. The snowball effect begins to take over, and each lie begets another lie. When these lies are accepted as truth, you begin to negatively speak to and about yourself.

Depression can be a result of believing these lies. Is there a heavy burden you carry around that is saying your value and worth are negligible or nonexistent?

What about anxiety? Are you apprehensive about everything? Do you spend a large part of your day worrying about "what if" scenarios that never happen? Are you stuck believing and worrying about a lie that never becomes truth but robs you of joy "in the moment?" Unfortunately, anxiety robs you of many moments.

As a counselor, I hear over and over about the impact that negative experiences have in the lives of my clients, and these experiences (and the lies they associate with them) have overtaken them emotionally.

If you grew up in a highly critical home, you may become paralyzed about taking risks, making decisions, or stepping out on your own for fear of failure or criticism. As life moves forward, we can't stand still; we must move, and that can begin to create anxiety. Fear is at the root of anxiety.

If you grew up in a home with substance abuse, then verbal (or physical or sexual) abuse may have accompanied that as well. The morning after, the abuser probably doesn't even remember what was said (or done), but it doesn't mean it didn't happen.

Because you know; you were there. It happened to you! The stories go on and on with domestic violence, physical and sexual abuse, abandonment, marital affairs, divorce, addictions, and broken homes.

These stories start with "someone else" doing or saying something to you. Now, that's not the real beginning—it's only the beginning you might know. The reality is, it started with the person before you, and with the person before him. Sometimes we know their story, but usually we don't.

## Everyone Is Flawed

Remember when I spoke of parents having good intentions? Well, here's another one of my stories—one of many when I was young child. I was born with what I was told were "webbed toes." Not just a simple web between all five toes—no, three of my toes were literally joined together as one large toe, yet there were three separate bones inside this massive toe. It didn't affect my ability to walk or run, but it sure looked different from my other foot.

Unfortunately, it also looked very different from the feet of other children in my neighborhood and school. I learned very early that children can be the cruelest creatures on the planet, and yet they are also the most susceptible to the teasing and taunting of their peers. I was no exception. I felt different, I felt hurt and made fun of, and I felt unaccepted.

Everyone I saw had perfect feet with all 10 toes. I remember hearing those words when someone had a new baby, and they would use that exact expression— "Yep, she has all 10 fingers and toes"—as if that was the standard to measure whether a child was healthy, perfect, or accepted.

Was I unhealthy? Was there something wrong with me because I didn't have 10 toes? I began to believe it. I began to believe the lie.

I always had a great relationship with my mom—I could talk to her on just about any subject. So one day, I told her the kids at school teased me about my foot. My mom cried when I told her, and explained something she had never told me. When she was newly pregnant with me, she became very sick. The doctors gave her some medicine and assured her it would not affect her baby. When I was born and she looked me over and found that I didn't have 10 toes, she cried out of guilt. Perhaps it was the medicine she had taken, my mom thought. She felt responsible for my deformed foot.

I never blamed her. Still, I remembered her saying she had counted my toes, so I believed there must be something important to having all 10 fingers and toes, otherwise why would every new parent do that?

So the adversary began to speak lies to me, saying that I didn't measure up; I had something wrong with me; I was damaged goods. When the lies first start coming at you, you can almost discern them, but then they keep coming. One after another. Unshielded from the devil, you feel every lie penetrate your soul, and you begin to weaken. Worse, you begin to walk in that lie.

Then my mom said something I'm sure she thought was going to be very helpful to me. But it wasn't—not for years to come.

She said, "Kim, no one is perfect. Everyone is flawed." Now, I didn't get a full explanation of what that meant. I was so young, I believed she was saying that everyone had some kind of physical defect. So, I began looking for them. I found myself evaluating everyone I met, wondering what their imperfections were. In most people, I couldn't find it. They all looked perfect and beautiful, and for sure I counted toes.

Now, my imperfection was my foot, but I walked and ran just fine. No one knew I had this problem unless I took off my shoes and socks.

Since my mom had said everyone was flawed, I began to believe that many people had secret deficiencies like mine. They weren't easily detectable. Sometimes those are the worst kind—the kind that are hidden, secret. I began to feel that at some point, when I became good friends with someone, I needed to "come clean" and tell them about my foot. Then I'd wait for their reaction to see if they too would be like the kids who teased me when I was younger.

But as I grew up, I learned what my mom was trying to tell me about how everyone was flawed. She didn't mean physically—she meant emotionally and spiritually flawed.

We are all sinners. We all have battles we struggle with, and trials to endure and overcome. How we respond to the enemy makes all the

difference in the quality of our lives. In any trial, there are two components: the trial itself and the gift of escape. In both components, God
provides for us if we allow Him to lead us.

We all have temptations, too, whether it's an extra piece of cake, or
something that doesn't belong to us, or sex, or drugs and alcohol. Mine
is carbs. Not just a few chips, but the entire bag—oh, and vanilla ice
cream.

Whatever the temptation is, it doesn't come from God.

> *Let no one say when he is tempted, "I am being tempted by God,"*
> *for God cannot be tempted with evil, and he himself tempts no one.*

James 1:13

Satan is the one who tempts us, and he uses our own weaknesses to do so.
In those moments of temptation, God will provide a way for you to escape
if you're looking for the way out. That is the key: you have to be looking
for a Godly way out.

And, of course, who do you think wants to distract you? Who do you
think continues to relentlessly hand you lie after lie about how you need
that which is tempting you? God will never leave you and His words are
true. But you won't feel God's influence unless you choose Him.

> *… God is faithful, and he will not let you be tempted beyond your*
> *ability, but with the temptation he will also provide the way of escape,*
> *that you may be able to endure it.*

1 Cor. 10:13

One thing is for sure: you can't do it alone. You can't do it unshielded and
unprotected. You need to learn how to put on the Armor of God. Without
it, you feel every sting, every wound, every kind of trauma, and the worst
of all is what happens to your mind. You believe every lie! Once you do,
your whole body believes it and follows it.

Let me give you my very own Psychology 101 Cliff Notes. There are four stages that characterize our path in life: Beliefs, Emotions, Actions, and Results. I nicknamed them B.E.A.R. Whatever you Believe (truth or lie), you feel (Emotions). You respond to those feelings with Actions. Those actions create Results, good or bad.

The key to having great results in life is to start with your beliefs. Now, I'm not just talking religion—I'm talking about anything you believe in. When God told us in Ephesians 6 that our battle is spiritual and not flesh and blood, does that mean we're fighting spirits and demons? Or does it mean something else?

I propose that what you are fighting is spiritual, and the battlefield you are on is in your mind. How would you define a thought? Is it flesh and blood, or spiritual? Can you see your thoughts, or touch them? No. A thought is like the wind: you cannot see it, but you can see its effects.

That is how the Spirit is defined:

> *The wind blows where it wishes, and you hear its sound, but you do not know where it comes from or where it goes. So it is with everyone who is born of the spirit.*

> John 3:8

Why am I talking about your thoughts? Because this is where your enemy attacks you. This is how your battle is spiritual. I'd like for you to take a step back for a moment and ponder what I am about to say.

The adversary has but one function here on earth: to convince you to believe his lies.

In the beginning, our adversary was named Lucifer, and he was with God in heaven as one of His most beautiful and powerful creatures. I believe Lucifer was present at the time of the master plan to create humans.

We now know Lucifer as Satan, our worst enemy. He is evil, but brilliant. He knows us, and he knows our weaknesses. He will use anything that is your weakness—whatever your own individual Achilles' heel—to get you to believe his lies.

And once you believe, you will respond to that lie with emotions that motivate your actions, and the result is chaos in your life.

I want you to step back—because sometimes when we are so close to a situation, we don't have a clear vision to see things as they really are. And, if you're spiritually and emotionally unprotected, you may struggle and reject the truth because it's too painful. That's another lie. Emotionally vulnerable, you close your eyes, retreat, avoid, lash out, hide under your covers, and hope it all goes away. Or worse, you believe the lies and begin to act on them.

If your life is not abundant, it usually didn't happen overnight. It took time—Satan implants his lies little by little. When you look at your life from a distance, notice the slow fade as a result of believing his lies: you're not good enough, you can't overcome your weaknesses, you don't have the strength to become what God wants you to be.

Doesn't it make you angry? Why do we give our worst enemy that power over us?

Acting on Satan's lies results in the ruined lives we see around us. For example, see the wife who listens to so many negative lies about herself that she runs to another man who speaks flattering words she longs to hear. She doesn't realize Satan is plotting to destroy her marriage. See the father who doesn't parent out of love, but instead restricts and punishes his child because he himself never felt loved as a child. See the abuser who believes she needs to control others to protect herself from being controlled and hurt. See the murderer who takes someone's life because he believes that person deserved it, or believes he is doing the world a favor by cleansing the impurities in it. See the addict who believes that drugs or alcohol are the only way to cope with misery and heartache.

Yes, it makes me angry. I'm not angry at people—I'm angry at where we are right now by believing the lies. Satan's plan is to kill and destroy, and he does it in a very cunning and crafty way.

No matter what negative thing we're experiencing in life, there are belief attachments, thoughts that are attached to things that are lies, yet we don't stop to seek the truth first. We haven't been taught to seek the truth before responding.

The beginning of understanding is to look for things you cannot see. It's a shift from physical to spiritual. It's an introduction to faith—the conviction of things not seen. Genuine faith has two parts: belief and action. First, you need to change your beliefs.

It's time to meet your real enemy.

# 2

## FATHER OF LIES

*… He was a murderer from the beginning, and does not stand in the truth, because there is no truth in him. When he lies, he speaks out of his own character, for he is a liar and the father of lies.*

*John 8:44*

### The Adversary's Beginning

Before Earth was created, God created angels, the most beautiful of whom was named Lucifer. Ezekiel gives us some details about him:

*You were an anointed guardian cherub. I placed you; you were on the holy mountain of God; in the midst of the stones of fire you walked. You were blameless in your ways from the day you were created, till unrighteousness was found in you.*

*Ezek. 28:14-15*

Lucifer was an anointed cherub and he lived with God on his holy mountain. Lucifer had it all. But what was this unrighteousness that was found in him? He became proud—as if any of his beauty and status were of his own making.

In verse 16, we continue to read that this anointed cherub was cast out of God's holy mountain. In verse 17, we learn that Lucifer's heart was proud because of his beauty, and his wisdom was corrupted and he was cast to the ground.

Isaiah 14:12 confirms Lucifer was fallen from heaven—but keep reading. Lucifer wasn't just prideful because he was made beautiful. Lucifer wanted to be God:

> *You said in your heart, "I will ascend to heaven; above the stars of God I will set my throne on high; I will sit on the mount of assembly in the far reaches of the north…"*

Isa. 14:13

We have to search several places in the Bible to put the full picture together of how Lucifer became Satan. Let's go back to the book of Revelation.

Like humans, angels were created with free will. Without it, we would be reduced to robots, doing nothing except what was internally designed for us to do. However, free will allows choices, and the choices God wants for all his creation is to choose Him. Free will, as much as that gets us into so much trouble, is a necessary part of creating a loving relationship.

Lucifer exercised his free will to rebel against God, but he wasn't the only one. When God threw Lucifer out of heaven, one third of all the angels were cast out with him. (Rev. 12:4) A third of how many? The Bible doesn't say. It does, however, give a glimpse of the magnitude of angels in heaven as God reveals in numerous stories the angels who are out there fighting with us.

After Lucifer's fall, his name was changed:

*And the great dragon was thrown down, that ancient serpent, who is called the devil and Satan, the deceiver of the whole world—he was thrown down to the earth, and his angels were thrown down with him.*

Rev. 12:9

It's vital you understand this story, because it holds the key to understanding why you are fighting so many battles. Look where Satan and his fallen angels (demons) ended up—they were cast out to Earth! Satan could not be the God of Heaven, but he certainly is the god of this world! Not just that, but he has an agenda, a scheme, to deceive the whole world:

*In their case the god of this world has blinded the minds of the unbelievers, to keep them from seeing the light of the gospel of the glory of Christ, who is the image of God.*

2 Cor. 4:4

Can you see what is happening?

I know you might be thinking, "Why is this even important to me? I don't care about Satan or his story. I've got enough problems and battles of my own to be concerned about him." That's exactly what Satan wants you to believe! He doesn't want you to understand his relevance in your life—because then you'll be onto him and his schemes.

See, there's something about truth you need to understand: once you know the truth, lies have no power over you, because you recognize they are false. So who is lying to you? The Adversary! If you know the truth, not only does the lie have no power over you, but get this: neither does the adversary! Satan does not want you to understand truth, and he has put his entire existence into creating and crafting the most outrageous lies using every weakness, temptation, or person we love or despise in order to get us to believe it.

Remember, that's all he needs to do. Once we believe his lies, we are on our own course of destruction and despair. Now, let me continue to unfold this story, and you will see the truth of what and whom you are truly battling.

Lucifer had it all except for one thing: he wanted to be God. When that failed, he set up his domain here, where he can be the god of this world. It's no wonder so many things are happening in our world that don't make sense, that are cruel, ugly, even horrific at times. Why is there so much hatred and destruction? Because of jealousy. If you are a child of God, Satan is jealous of YOU! That's right. Satan despises and is jealous of anyone in God's favor. If you are not yet in His favor, then the devil is doing everything he can to distract you from turning to God and wearing His armor.

Because of the choices Satan made, he can no longer reign with the Father and the Son forever. His home is no longer Heaven. When God began to implement his creation plan, there was a hierarchy and order of function and of power. The function and power is related to the hierarchy of angels over humans. Angels are created above humans in knowledge and in power at this time.

One function of an angel is to minister to the saints—to those who believe in Jesus!

*Are they not all ministering spirits sent out to serve for the sake of those who are to inherit salvation?*

Heb. 1:14

*For He will command His angels concerning you to guard you in all your ways.*

Ps. 91:11

<u>The Adversary's Schemes</u>
Satan is deceptive and manipulating. He is the master at twisting truth into a lie. He has managed to deceive even some of those who appear to be Christian leaders. This might be a hard saying, but where does the Bible say you will find a "false prophet?"

> *But false prophets also arose among the people, just as there will be false teachers among you, who will secretly bring in destructive heresies, even denying the Master who bought them, bringing upon themselves swift destruction.*

2 Pet. 2:1

Who are these people?

> *For such men are false apostles, deceitful workmen, disguising themselves as apostles of Christ. And no wonder, for even Satan disguises himself as an angel of light. So it is no surprise if his servants, also, disguise themselves as servants of righteousness. Their end will correspond to their deeds.*

2 Cor. 11:13-15

Satan and his servants have changed themselves into something that "seems" right—even righteous—yet they are fake and extremely powerful:

> *Beware of false prophets, who come to you in sheep's clothing but inwardly are ravenous wolves.*

Matt. 7:15

Satan's intention is to knock you off track, to keep you guessing and to keep you confused. In fact, these false prophets and false Christs are so cunning and slick, it can be hard for even those who really study God's word to not be fooled:

> *For false Christs and false prophets will arise and perform great signs and wonders, so as to lead astray, if possible, even the elect.*

Matt. 24:24

We can only begin to see our battles with clarity when we understand that all the craziness in our lives does not come either from God or people, but from the craftiness of the devil. God wants us to fully understand Satan's schemes:

> *So that we may no longer be children, tossed to and fro by the waves and carried about by every wind of doctrine, by human cunning, by craftiness in deceitful schemes.*

Eph. 4:14

In fact, Satan is such a good liar, he devises these schemes to be so attractive that we believe we need or must follow them.

> *See, this alone I found, that God made man upright, but they have sought out many schemes.*

Eccles. 7:29

God doesn't create "schemes." No, in fact, he's the complete opposite.

> *For God is not a God of confusion but of peace...*

1 Cor. 14:33

He speaks truth, and His truth is what guides our lives if we allow it to. God wants His children to walk uprightly, to know what is right and good, and to recognize when the hand of the devil is at play—and then for us to hand the devil TRUTH. Truth is our weapon! Once truth is spoken, there is nothing else to say.

If you do not know truth, you will believe a lie. If you know the truth, however, not only do lies have no power over you, but if you speak the truth back to the liars, one of two things happen: liars either a) remain silent because the truth puts them in their place (you're on to them), or b) they attempt to run another set of lies by you.

Let's go to the story of Jesus after his 40-day fast, where the devil was talking smack to Jesus. What did Jesus do? He spoke truth, he spoke scripture, and Satan chose option B. He moved from one lie to another—from offering Jesus the world if He would bow down to him, to trying to get Jesus to tempt His father by throwing Himself off the mountain. When Jesus finally got tired of Satan's shenanigans, He told Satan to get behind Him! There was nothing left to say. And, notice this, after Satan left,

> *...angels came and were ministering to Him.*

> Matt. 4:11

Jesus had had enough. The lies had no power over Jesus, and they don't have any power over us, either. We just need a new Belief (remember B.E.A.R.).

Do you ever feel sometimes like trouble seems to find you? You might not be that far off when you say that. Here's why:

> *Be sober-minded; be watchful. Your adversary the devil prowls around like a roaring lion, seeking someone to devour.*

> I Pet. 5:8

## Know What You Are Fighting

It seems like when we're engaged in a battle, we focus on the physical parts. We look at people or things or situations, and we get so angry at how people can say and do things to hurt us. But now you understand that you aren't fighting the physical.

That's one of the lies—one of the biggest lies we believe. Nope, the physical part is just the tool. Most of us haven't learned enough about the spiritual to discern this.

> *For we do not wrestle against flesh and blood, but against the rulers, against the authorities, against the cosmic powers over this present darkness, against the spiritual forces of evil in the heavenly places.*

> Eph. 6:12

I don't know about you, but that seems like a battle way over my head. Oh, did you catch that? There's the little lie—do you see how cunning he is? If it's too much for us, too over the top, way out of our ability to understand, then we tend to disregard it, almost as if it's someone else's responsibility. It's for someone else to figure out.

Or is it? Because guess what—you're walking in it. No matter what, you're walking in something. Either you're walking in truth, or you're walking in a lie. It's important you know which!

So to whom are you listening? I always want to give a plug, a shout-out to anyone I come across who totally understands this question. I love the book *Battlefield of the Mind* by Joyce Meyer. It's an excellent read about how the adversary gets into our heads and surrounds us with all kinds of lies and, as he hands us his gift of deception, we willingly accept it and embrace it all as our own!

No! These are not our lies, they are not truth, and he is not a sheep. He is not the Lamb, he is a wolf, masquerading as something innocent to lure you into his destructive lies.

The Lies You Believe

In all my years of counseling practice, this area is the hardest for me to penetrate. Remember B.E.A.R., the acronym I gave you earlier? B = Belief, where everything starts. Belief is what determines the direction of your actions, and the results of your life all stem from your beliefs.

Here is truth: God tells us He has a plan for each and every one of us, a plan to prosper us, and to give us a more abundant life, not just in this world, but in the world to come. This isn't the truth that people in my office walk in. It might not be the truth you walk in, either. So what lies do you believe to be truth? What lies have you accepted as your own?

Because so many of the lies go back into childhood, they have become a part of who we think we are, and the results in our lives tell that story in the form of anxiety, low self-worth, depression, suicidal ideation, promiscuity, anger, rebellion, and the list can go on and on.

Do any of the things I just listed sound like a prosperous and abundant life? No, they are just the opposite. The adversary has been successful to kill, steal, and destroy the quality of so many lives. Over the years, I've heard so many lies my clients are walking in that I created a list below. You just might find some of your lies in here.

Satan's Lies That We Receive as Our Truth

I'm not good enough / I'll never be good enough / No one loves me / No one will ever love me / I am damaged / No one will ever want me / I am unlovable / I can't trust anyone / Everyone is untrustworthy / I hate myself / I am stupid / I've done so many bad things God will not forgive me / I can't ask for forgiveness / I don't deserve to be forgiven / I can't do anything right / Everything I do is wrong / It doesn't matter what I do, I'll never get it right / I am ugly / Why should I keep trying. . . it's not going to make a difference / Who cares, anyway / No one understands me / If I'm as good as God says I am,  then why did my parent leave me? / I've hurt too many people—no one will accept me back/ If I killed myself no one would even miss me / Everyone's life would be better if I just killed myself / I am a loser. . .

This list could go on and on.

Did you find a lie on the list that you've believed? Or perhaps you found yourself in many of them? So you see, thoughts are spiritual. You cannot see them or touch them, but you can see and feel their consequences. This is the spiritual battle Ephesians 6 is talking about!

We can look at the destruction of our world everywhere, yet we do not recognize "who" is doing the destroying. We think it's about the other guy—your partner, your kids, your boss, the hostile customer, the other country, and we look at all of them as the enemy, but as you have just learned, none of them is the true enemy.

Satan is our enemy and lies are his tools of deception. Once you believe the lie, he sets in motion the path for your life! Look around you. The world is crazy and out of control, but people are not the enemy—no, they are only a pawn in the devil's chess game of life. You are a pawn as well—but no longer!

The Accuser

How can you tell if these negative thoughts are yours or the adversary's? You may have lived with these thoughts your entire life. You may have grown accustomed to not just the thoughts, but the actions that follow them as well.

There's a way to know whether what you are thinking is true or false—from God or from the devil. Godly thoughts are not filled with accusations. Godly thoughts are not condemning (toward self or others). He has given us examples to follow.

Remember the woman at the well? She was accused of adultery, and the penalty back then was to be stoned to death. Jesus, in His wisdom, asks her accusers to cast the first stone, yet there was a qualifier: only those who had no sin could participate. Silence. That's truth, and that's what happens when you speak truth. There's nothing left to say on the subject. Especially when someone knows it's truth.

Have you ever been accused of something you didn't do? How about when your intentions were undermined? Have you ever felt condemned in the midst of doing what you thought was right? How about being on the receiving end of finger-pointing, blaming, and even comments from people who think they know more than you about your motives and intentions? Oh, does that get to me!

That reminds me of some triggers I experienced years ago. I always looked at myself as a more logical person when it came to responding to things, or making decisions. I was probably more of a literal thinker than what was actually good for me, and for those who were around me.

This was certainly true when it came to helping out my sister, Terrie, years ago. Remember earlier in this book, I spoke about temperament and how different temperaments respond in unique ways?

Our story makes me think of Cain and Abel. There wasn't enough detail to know if the brothers bantered with each other, or whether Cain silently brewed and simmered his anger to the boiling point. One thing was sure, at some point Cain believed a lie, and was thoroughly enraged at his brother for doing what seemed like innocent obedience. Cain fostered anger and resentment against his brother to the point of killing him in a field.

I'm glad my story doesn't end like that, but I believed there were some similarities between the Cain and Abel story and the story of Terrie and me. She wasn't obedient. That is truth. The "why" is something we'll never know. I was obedient, but I didn't have *Godly* obedience. Godly obedience is where you surrender your heart and soul and will to the Lord. Godly obedience doesn't focus on self at all; it is outward-focused on God and those around you.

No, my obedience was more from fear than surrender. I want to speak truth here, so don't think I'm saying I was like Abel. The common factor in my story and Abel's is that my sister was jealous of me just as Cain was jealous of Abel. Terrie made some choices in her life based on her beliefs—or rather, based on lies she accepted about herself—and specifically about who she thought I was. I'm not sure when exactly this division began to take place, but it was very early in our childhood.

She called me "the good one"—as in, I was the good child and she was the one who did everything wrong. She took every opportunity to point that out to me, usually right after she'd had some negative fallout from choices she had made based on false beliefs.

The spiral in life continues if you are not aware of what is happening, and it was the same between my sister and me. It was true we made different choices, but certainly not because I was "the good one." No, I was the flawed one. I was the one with only eight toes. I was the one constantly searching for acceptance.

My beliefs were just as wrong as Terrie's, yet our actions in life created very different results. Unfortunately, the results in her life left her always wanting for something—for enough food for her and her children, for enough money to make ends meet, and for recognition other than what she believed herself to be: a failure.

My sister measured her failures against my successes, and the distance between us continued to grow. I found I could not share my successes with her because I worried she would think I was rubbing her nose in it, so I stopped sharing.

However, that didn't stop the resentment from growing. I never doubted Terrie's love for me, but I struggled to *feel* her love toward me, if that makes any sense. Other people told me she spoke kindly of me, and even bragged sometimes, but she would never directly say those words to me.

Has this ever happened to you with people you care about? The wedge began to take on a life of its own. At the time, I did not understand it or recognize it for what it was, so being completely exposed emotionally, I responded in the flesh. I was completely vulnerable to the accusations of the devil (not my sister), and the division grew wider.

I wasn't trying to be good; I was merely trying to be accepted. Perhaps if I excelled, I thought, then people wouldn't notice the speech impediment or know that I had this secret number of toes by which parents measured perfection. My sister didn't know me at all, yet she thought she did. I didn't know her either, but I responded to her as though I did.

Terrie and I could never seem to get on the same page, even though internally I believe we fought very similar negative thoughts. It was as though neither of us could move out of our comfort zone to truly see the other person.

My stance in life seemed to make Terrie's inadequacies stand out, as though all her mistakes were written with a permanent highlighter. The lies we both believed cheated us out of a great relationship with each other. We were not each other's enemy—Satan was.

We're not alone here. Have you ever been afraid to move forward because you're afraid of the unknown? Because going forward took you out of your comfort zone? I know from the stories in Exodus that the Israelites felt that way as well. Remember when they were being led out of Egypt? Everyone was so excited to get out of town until they were met with obstacles. Yes, they were big obstacles, given that the Red Sea was in front of them, and a Pharaoh who had changed his mind about letting them go was behind them, and he was in hot pursuit to bring all the Israelites back into captivity (Ex. 14:11-12).

Unfortunately, we can be just like the Israelites. We too can get comfortable in our negative situations—not because we like being in them, but because the fear of the unknown can sometimes feel worse.

It was a faith issue for the Israelites thousands of years ago, and it's probably a faith issue for you and me today. It certainly was a faith issue for my sister and me. Faith is about believing what you do not see. Once you stand in faith, it's incredible how much more you actually do see.

Beware though, because the devil wants you right where you are. He is the one that doesn't want you to change. How many times have you been sick and tired and started to make changes? Here come the lies FULL FORCE!

They are negative accusations, allegations, and wrongful intentions, and the adversary has permeated your thought processes to cast doubt, fear, envy, etc. Maybe you've even begun to develop buyer's remorse. You may ask yourself, "What have I done? I shouldn't have attempted this! I'm only making the situation worse! I should just stay where I am!"

When this happens, you have bought into the lies, and the adversary has fully convinced you that 1) these thoughts are yours, and 2) that they are truth! *Both* are lies! Instead of going full steam ahead, we find ourselves in a cowardly position, retreating, head down, and fully accepting failure. Am I right?

No, I'm not a fly on your wall. I've just become keenly aware of the adversary's schemes. I wasn't always. I've been where you are more times than I like to admit. Sometimes I can find myself right back there. Yes, I've stood completely vulnerable, over and over again and I've felt the impact of the devil's fiery arrows penetrate to my very core. That is, until I became aware of the power of God's Armor.

When our good intentions are attacked and we are not clothed in Armor, human nature's response is to counter-attack and defend ourselves. In the flesh, that seems to make perfect sense. How dare that person tell me what my intentions are! They have no idea what I'm thinking! Guess what—you're absolutely right. They don't. Why can't we rest in that truth? Because the adversary doesn't want us to rest. Because in rest, there is no quarrel, there is no fight, there is no anger. He loses, and he hates to lose.

What would this kind of battle look like if you had your armor on? Jesus gives a great example of how he responded to all the haters of his day. Remember what he said? "Forgive them Father, for they know not what they do!" Do you think Jesus had the right to defend himself? Sure! Do you think his motives were pure? Absolutely! But he did not enter into that dark place. He actively chose not to enter into the ring with Satan, and we need to learn how to stay out of that ring as well.

To recap: you are magnificently made in God's image. He has a plan for you—a plan to give us an abundant life, and to prosper. You also have an enemy who is highly jealous of who and what you are. He has blinded you to truth so that you walk in lies. Those lies bring emotional destruction as you play them out as though they are truth.

You know who your enemy is now. It's time to become a warrior walking in truth. Before any war is to be waged, a warrior must become prepared. Let's prepare.

# 3

# THE WARRIOR

*The LORD is my rock, and my fortress and my deliverer; my God, my rock in whom I take refuge, my shield, and the horn of my salvation, my stronghold and my refuge, my savior; you save me from violence. I call upon the LORD who is worthy to be praised, and I am saved from my enemies.*

*2 Sam. 22:2-4*

When I think of a Biblical warrior, what comes to mind is David fighting Goliath. David was a young kid, and Goliath was a giant. David didn't have skills or experience, but he sure had heart. A few stones and a sling-shot—and the colossal giant was dead.

I relate to David because I, too, am small. I'm 5 feet nothing. Every 12-year-old is taller than me, and it seems many of my battles are like fighting Goliath. They all seem so much bigger than I am! But, like David, I was a scrapper.

I grew up in Detroit in the '70s. I went to a school that was 90% African-American where racial fighting was at an all-time high, and our school seemed to use busing and riots as the answer. High school was a test of endurance. For whatever reason, I came into my own then. I became confident and self-assured. I got into fights (and won), and like that young David, I had heart. I started learning that showing up for the fight was half the battle.

The mental fight is the hardest. Your feet follow your thoughts, and I wanted my feet going in a positive direction. I graduated high school with honors. Now, that's not to say I was smart. In fact, I always teased myself that I thought many of the teachers gave me a passing grade just for being brave enough to show up.

One thing is for sure: character isn't developed when life is easy. Franklin D. Roosevelt says it this way: "A smooth sea never made a skilled sailor." Isn't it funny that a counter to that is, "Don't rock the boat" or "Don't make waves"? Who would've thought that what those phrases really mean is "Stay unskilled" or "Stay weak"?

God talks about how trials transform us into what He wants us to be. He has given us everything we need to be successful. He tells us that many places throughout the Bible:

> *To those who have obtained a faith of equal standing with ours by the righteousness of our God and Savior Jesus Christ; May grace and peace be multiplied to you in the knowledge of God and of Jesus our Lord.*

> 2 Pet. 1:1-2

In this same passage a little further down, Peter describes a process we go through for growth and change:

> *For this very reason, make every effort to supplement your faith with virtue, and virtue with knowledge, and knowledge with self-control, and self-control with steadfastness, and steadfastness with godliness, and godliness with brotherly affection, and brotherly affection with love.*

> 2 Pet. 1:5-7

It starts small, and builds over time. This may be all new to you or may be a refresher, but you are designed to be a powerful spiritual warrior. It is your destiny.

Silver has to go through the fire before it can show a reflection, and so do we. We must go through the fire of life's trials to hone our skills to reflect an image that looks like Jesus. We don't go "around" or "over" or "under" the fire—we must go through it. To become a well-trained soldier, we must practice our skills. To become a skillful spiritual warrior, we need to go through the trial.

## Free Will

As a young girl, I never understood the idea of free will, nor did I understand why God created us with a human nature that would instinctively go against Him. In fact, because of my ignorance, the idea that God would create humans with free will, and design our nature to be against Him, actually made me angry.

Why would He do that? Why would He make our life here on earth so difficult? Now, I know the created shouldn't question the Creator, but I was a kid needing answers. I finally got that answer when I became a mother (all in God's good timing).

Here is how my answer unfolded. If you're a parent, then you will appreciate this analogy. Not only does this analogy give me the answer I sought as a child, it also outlines our Christian growth. I love how stories in the Bible have duality, and I especially love how God allowed this duality to play out in the answer I was seeking.

I discovered this analogy in three different stages, and each of these stages unfolds our spiritual journey. I'll identify the physical issue before I match it with its spiritual counterpart.

### Stage One:

If your child's DNA were embedded with an ability to clean his room, would a clean room mean anything to you? If you're a parent, I know you're smiling right now, as what parent doesn't have "clean your room" battles?

I can tell you, as a mother of four children, the dirty-room battle is real!! Now, it might sound wonderful to have a built-in "clean-room gene," because your child would—instinctively, without nagging—always clean his room. In fact, this subject wouldn't even be an issue. Just like breathing, cleaning would be something that just happens naturally.

But since we know our children do not have a "clean your room" gene, we need to go to the next stage of discovery.

*Stage Two:*

If your child cleans his room for no other reason than to get a reward or not be punished, would you be happy that he cleaned his room? Perhaps a little, since it's better than a dirty room, but you're not very satisfied with why he did it.

It's a very selfish motive, right? When a child cleans his room just to get a reward or to avoid discipline, the motive is selfish and not internally driven. External motives like these are short-lived, and if the reward or punishment isn't big enough for them, the motivation diminishes or dies, or the child begins to up the ante with manipulation and bartering.

As parents, we would need to constantly be monitoring the reward/punishment system, and what happens if we actually forget to give them either? Our words lose their power, and the child's motivation decreases even more. Now, let's talk about the final stage.

*Stage Three:*

Imagine your child goes into his room and cleans it—for no other reason than wanting to please you—and then says to you, "Hey, come here. I want to show you something." He takes you by the hand and leads you into his room and cheerfully says, "I cleaned my room for you!"

Now, granted, this doesn't happen very often, but as a parent, what would you want to do for this child at this moment? ANYTHING! Right? In fact, anytime our children do something for no other reason than to please us, we are almost speechless, our hearts are bursting with joy, and we have an overwhelming desire to shower them with our blessings.

This analogy, discovered during my mom-tantrums of wanting a clean room, is how I got my answer to why we humans are not designed by nature to love God. This analogy also explains most of our early Christian journey, our spiritual conversion as Christians.

Just as a child's DNA is not embedded with a longing to clean his room, our DNA is not designed with a natural desire to love God. It is not in our human nature to do things to please him. The natural man, in fact, is an enemy to God:

> *For the mind that is set on the flesh is hostile to God, for it does not submit to God's law; indeed, it cannot.*

Rom. 8:7

Just as a child learns about reward and punishment, we begin to understand the concept of Heaven and Hell, blessings and cursings, and with our selfish motives we'll do righteous-looking things to either get the reward to go to Heaven or to not get the punishment of going to Hell.

Our motives, however, are just like most children's: self-oriented. God knows our motives, and obedience is just the beginning of conversion. What He is really looking for is our complete surrender of our will to His.

When we finally move beyond selfish intentions and understand the kind of loving relationship God is looking for, just like *our* children who do things to please us, we move from the law of "shalt-nots" into loving obedience and surrender to please God.

So why am I talking about free will in the Warrior chapter? Because free will is at the heart of all our decisions. Whether we choose to make decisions that move us closer to God or further away, it's about our ability to choose.

As this book begins to unfold, we need to build on our understanding chapter by chapter. So, let's recap just a bit.

All of us have believed lies and have responded to them in negative ways, and those responses have not served us well.

Perhaps you have the gift of discernment and the lies you agree with and own are minimal. If so, you are one of the lucky ones. Perhaps you haven't honed that skill very well. Maybe you can recognize you have believed many lies. Maybe you have blamed many people for your misery or misfortune, you have acted upon those lies, and some aspects of your life are in chaos.

Wherever you find yourself at this very moment, recognize this is a pivotal shift in your life going forward. This begins the release of chains that have been weighing you down. This is where the rubber meets the road and truth is in the driver's seat.

No longer are you going to let yourself be naked and vulnerable to the attacks of Satan. Will he still try? Oh yes. Will you feel his attacks? Yes, you will. But you will be armored, you will have truth, and you will become a skillful warrior.

Free will: it means the choice is yours. You're reading this book because the subject intrigued you, or perhaps you're a supportive friend or family member. However you came to read this, my hope is that your eyes are open to truth and your heart rejects the lies.

Bad things happen. They just do. That's truth. It's when bad things happen to us and we can't *move on* that problems begin. It's when we're locked onto the physical things in our lives instead of the spiritual that we lose our focus.

When strongholds feel like they are too much to handle, we begin to take matters into our own hands to fix the problem. Even when we think we have a clear understanding of the promises of God, we can get tripped up. No one is immune to this; everyone can be deceived. Abraham and Sarah had this very problem. Remember the promise God made to Abraham? Abraham was going to have a son, and through Abraham his seeds would be as the stars in the sky.

Patience is something I believe most people struggle with, and depending on the topic or subject, I have plenty or none at all. Patience was Sarah's problem, too. She couldn't wait for God to give her a child of her own, so she offered Hagar, her handmaiden to Abraham.

There! That's what God must have meant! "Abraham, you can take Hagar and *she* can give us a son." That's exactly what happened, and Abraham had a son named Ishmael—but this was not the son God was speaking of. No, that son was Isaac. His birth was a miracle from God to a woman who was almost 100 years old. But there's a lot more to this story: a story of jealousy, of division and separation of father and son, and a division between brothers.

This and countless other stories laid out for us in the Bible show that when we take matters into our own hands, the ending of the story is something quite different than what God had designed for us. When we insist on *our* will, we will find ourselves detoured from the path He wanted us to be on—the one He designed for us.

Lord knows, I have been on my fair share of detours. The journey always seems to start great, but the longer you're on that detour, the darker the path becomes. The straight road starts winding, unclear forks and decisions pop up, and soon it becomes difficult to know which way to turn. Have you ever been on a detour? Maybe you're on one right now.

If you're like me, or Abraham and Sarah, or a host of others who prophets have written about for our learning pleasure, the journey is long. I'm thinking about the Israelites right now, who really should have been on about an 11-day journey, but their detour (due to the hardening of their hearts) lasted 40 years wandering around the desert.

I don't know about you, but I want the shortest distance. Eleven days instead of 40 years; waiting on the Lord instead of creating chaos due to my lack of patience. I do know the shortest distance between two points is not necessarily the "easiest" path to take. That's how we get tripped up. God never said his path would be easy, but He did say it would be worth it, and that we would never be alone on the journey.

So back to free will and our ability to choose. Do you want to be a skilled warrior? Not a physical soldier, but a spiritual warrior. God has given you spiritual armor, spiritual weapons, and instructions to become a skillful and mighty warrior.

Most importantly, He has identified who the REAL enemy is. The choice is yours. Free will. This assignment, should you choose to accept it, will become one of the greatest changes and challenges in your life.

Faith

Glad to see you're still with me. Excellent!

Work Smarter, Not Harder. We've all heard this saying, but how does that apply to your specific challenge? Remember who is trying to knock you off center? The adversary doesn't want you to work smarter—he wants you to work harder. So hard that you just give up because it seems completely impossible. Sadly, many people do. SATAN wins . . . and the cycle continues over and over.

This is all going to stop! Today, right now! His game is up, we know his schemes, and we are on to him. He has you focused on the physical problems to distract you from what the real struggle actually is.

But today, we're taking a different look at this. We are gaining a new perspective on what is really happening, and with that perspective we become ARMED. Armed and dangerous to the adversary!

So what does working smarter mean? It means we take a spiritual look at our situation. We look beyond what we see and into what we can't. It's not as difficult as it sounds.

What exactly is faith?

> *Now faith is the assurance of things hoped for, the conviction of things not seen.*

Heb. 11:1

Most of us know this passage, but how many LIVE it?

Hebrews 11 is called the faith chapter because it identifies many people who stepped out in faith. Here is something I'd like you to ponder. We all want miracles in our life, right? We see miracles happen all around us, either people we know or read about in the news or watch on TV.

We can read about miracles in the Bible as well, and there is one thing specific to each and every case. Before every miracle, someone stepped out in faith. Someone walked out boldly onto the battlefield.

Do you know why this is a key piece of the puzzle? What part of B.E.A.R. does this resemble? Remember the acronym from the previous chapter? This is the Psychology 101 cliff notes: Beliefs, Emotions, Actions, Results = B.E.A.R.

Faith is the "B." We need faith to believe in something we cannot see. We cannot trust our own understanding.

> *Trust in the Lord with all your heart, and do not lean on your own understanding.*

> Prov. 3:5

What is truth? We can't find it in the world, nor can we rely on humans to tell us truth. We must rely on God's word, which is truth, and then walk in it. Our actions give testimony to what we believe, whether we live by faith and truth or we believe and walk in lies.

We find all kinds of examples of people who walked in faith, even though they could not see the outcome. Abraham was willing to kill his only son, Isaac, because he believed God. That story above all others pulls at my heart.

It is heartwrenching on several levels. I know how much Abraham and Sarah wanted a child, and Sarah had to wait until she was almost 100 years old before God granted them a son. When I've waited and anticipated something for a long time, that thing becomes so precious to me once I've received it. I can't imagine those feelings if it were a child I'd been waiting for. I know there are many people, maybe even you reading this, who have waited a very long time to have a child. That gift is powerful, and we become so attached to that child the very moment we conceive or adopt. The idea that God asked Abraham to kill his son stings me in a very real way. I know how much I love my own son, and to think of being asked to kill him sickens me to the core. Then I look at Abraham and his faith.

I don't read anywhere in the story where he lamented, cried, and wept uncontrollably (as I would have done). No, in fact, what I do read is the exact opposite. When Abraham was taking Isaac up to Mount Moriah to build the altar to sacrifice his son, Abraham was also with two others who accompanied them on the journey. When they got close, Abraham told them to wait. But notice what he says:

> *"Stay here with the donkey; I and the boy will go over there and worship and come again to you."*

Gen. 22:5

Put yourself where Abraham is right now. He is on his way to sacrifice his son—yet he is telling these men to wait for both of them to return after they worship.

We know that Abraham is the father of faith, so we can only guess what he might be thinking here. Either he believes God will not have him sacrifice his son, or he knows that even if he does have to, God has the power to raise him again.

This story pulls at my heartstrings every time I read it. I have a son I, too, prayed to receive. Abraham didn't present himself as a lamenting father, or even reveal to these men what God's intention was for him on that mountain. No, Abraham was fully armored, and most importantly, he showed up on the battlefield ready to fight. The battle is the Lord's, but we must show up for the fight. The faith Abraham had in God and in understanding his word is staggering to me.

The character of the people in the book of Hebrews shows they were warriors. They were engaged in what God wanted them to do, and I am confident they were fully armored in faith, not emotion. The key to miracles in our lives is our action of faith. I don't know of a single story in the Bible where miracles happened without a human bravely stepping out in faith first. Here are some examples.

Why did Cain hate his brother? Because Abel walked in faith. We know he did because his name is entered into the faith chapter, Hebrews 11. Abel believed God, and he walked in faith and gave an offering to God that expressed his understanding and love for God. Cain's offering, however, was not accepted. What does that mean? It means we can't just "go through the motions." Faith is at the core of who we are, and it's at the core of who God sees. When we become connected with God in this way, it IS powerful, and acting through our faith can move mountains.

Moses led the people out of Egypt without knowing where he was going. This man experienced God in a manner that paved the way for others to walk with God as well. From seeing the burning bush, to hearing God's words on the mountain, to carrying the tablets of stone written by the very hand of God, Moses moved in faith.

Moses didn't start out fully armored. No, he responded just like us, with fear and resistance. Moses did not want to be the spokesman because of his speech impediment. Maybe Moses couldn't say his Rs either!

Then, as the story unfolds, you can almost watch the transformation from a fearful man into a warrior. You can see his faith arise in how he carried the staff and how he engaged with the most powerful Pharaoh in the land. You can see his leadership emerge as he instructed everyone to kill a lamb and smear the blood on the doorpost to save their firstborn. Moses *acted* in faith and so did those Israelites, and miracles happened!

Moses's faith in following God helped lead more than a million men, women, and children out of slavery. The parting of the Red Sea, a miracle beyond miracles, didn't happen until Moses acted in faith and raised the staff. Can you see this theme over and over again? We must act in faith in order for our lives to miraculously change!

Did he stay armored? No, he didn't. He let the whiny Israelites get to him, and he became frustrated, and ultimately his response to striking the rock for water—in a way contrary to what God asked him to do—resulted in Moses not entering into the promised land with Joshua. It wasn't just Moses who didn't enter—all those whiny Israelites over the age of 20 didn't go in, either. They did not walk in faith, even though they saw unbelievable crazy miracles and signs of the hand of God.

How about Jonah, who was led to Nineveh to preach without knowing what would happen. Jonah didn't start out fully armored, either. Oh, no. Remember his story? He hid on a boat, trying to hide from God. When God has a plan for you, hiding doesn't tend to work well, and this story is an example. If you don't know or remember the story, then let me paraphrase it for you, Snyder-style.

Jonah needed a little convincing that God's plan was bigger and better than his own. I love this story because I see myself in Jonah. Even when reading the story, things are very clear what God wants him to do, but it wasn't in Jonah's plan, nor was it in Jonah's will. So he did what most of us do: he ran. Jonah hid, and denied his calling: "No, not me, God. No, I don't think so, God." Jonah considered the people of Nineveh to be enemies, and like us sometimes when we feel someone deserves punishment, he felt they should be punished, and wanted them to die in their sins. God wanted Jonah to go warn them, to give them another chance to change their ways.

Jonah ran away from God and away from his calling. He escaped on a boat, and was in the middle of the sea when a huge storm approached. What I find interesting in this story is that the other people on the boat didn't view this storm as just a random storm, like we would view it. No, they understood this storm to be the angry hand of God. (Side note: I always thought that was interesting. It's as if everything has a Godly purpose, including this storm, and these fishermen knew it!) After a while, these men had had enough of this storm, and they began to quiz Jonah. So, that begs a question: Are all the storms you experience just random storms, or is the hand of God trying to say something to you? Is God trying to get your attention?

What about Noah? Have you ever felt like him? Have you ever attempted to tell someone the truth over and over and not be heard? Or worse, ridiculed and mocked for your beliefs? If you've felt that, then Noah is you! The difference is, Noah was the only righteous person left on the earth. I can't imagine how alone he really must have felt. I'm not talking about on the boat—I'm talking about in his life on earth. The world had turned so far against God and God's ways that it had become very dark.

Noah didn't fit in with the world, or the world's beliefs and viewpoints, and certainly not the world's actions. Those differences separated Noah from the world—spiritually, intellectually, and certainly physically.

Another side note: Sadly, this reminds me of my relationship with my sister. She tended to use drugs as her escape, starting when she was about 15 years old. It wasn't consistent, but when things in her life became more than she could handle, drugs were her method of avoidance. Have you ever been around someone who was high or drunk when you were completely straight and sober? You can't relate to them. They make no sense intellectually, and sometimes their emotions and behaviors can be inappropriate or downright abusive. In Noah's story, it wasn't just a sibling, it was the whole world that made no sense. You, too, might feel like those around you make no sense. If so, then just like Noah, and like me sometimes, it can be very lonely.

What about the New Testament stories? How about the woman who was healed from a blood issue she'd had for years? Just by touching the hem of Christ's garment, she was healed. Jesus told her she was healed "by her faith." If she had not believed, or hadn't believed strongly enough to act on it, that miracle would not have happened.

I love all these stories. God put them in his book for a reason, and that reason is to show he can take imperfect people and cloak them with his armor to do amazing things! These stories are not for us to read and think that God moved in miraculous ways for *them*! No, he gave us these stories so we could see the human side of everyone he picked. We could see the flaws, the weakness, and the fear. He gave us these stories so we could see *us* in them.

These stories start out with people just like us, but then something happens. They transform from being fearful to emerging as powerful warriors! These aren't "super people" God selected. These people in the Bible are just like you and me; weak, fearful, willful, and, for some, not able to say their Rs. These people moved from their focus on the physical struggles to their focus on the spiritual; they moved out boldly in faith despite not knowing the outcome, for they believed God had a plan, and would help them complete their mission. Faith put into action creates the craziest unexplainable results in our life! The timing isn't ours to know "when" the results will happen. But, faith says IT WILL HAPPEN in God's timing!

Truth

> *For the time is coming when people will not endure sound teaching, but having itching ears they will accumulate for themselves teachers to suit their own passions, and will turn away from listening to the truth and wander off into myths.*

2 Tim. 4:3-4

Truth is a double-edged sword. It's difficult for us to function in life if we are heavily weighed down with the lies of the adversary. It can be downright exhausting listening to the negativity dance around in our heads. It can also be difficult to hear truth, especially if truth pricks our hearts or suggests we need to fix or change something. We want the easy way, the wide road. We don't like change, especially if we actually believe we are better off right where we are.

The deceptive part of a lie or a temptation is the glossy finish that is on every single thing that puts us on the detoured path. If we could see these distractions with the same clarity our Heavenly Father sees them, we would hate them and be repulsed, and we certainly would not be attracted, enticed, or tempted by them. We would be fully armored against the adversary's fiery arrows.

But we have to be ready for truth in order to hear it. God's truth changes everything. It brings meaning into our lives, gives clarity to what and whom we are fighting, and gives instructions for how to engage in the battles we fight daily.

Until we are ready for truth, we live in the lie, respond in the lie, and stay broken. One of the greatest lies is trying to work things out where "we" don't actually have to change. In fact, if we can change the laws of the land, and we could get people to accommodate "us" instead of going through the work to change ourselves, wouldn't that be much better? I ask this question, believing people logically will say "no," yet our society's behavior is actually saying, "YES!"

When you need to make a decision, do you gather all the naysayers, or do you collect all those who are in agreement with you, all those who are supportive and say all the right things that make you feel warm and fuzzy about your decision?

Believe it or not, better decisions are made when you listen to the naysayers. Yep—here's why. At some point, you've made the decision to go left instead of right. Making that decision came because you decided you needed or wanted to do something. The reality is, you don't need anyone on your side telling you it's a great decision (unless you're not sure it is, in which case, you probably haven't done your due diligence).

When you're making a decision, you need people who are not on your side. The opinions of those opposing you offer perspectives you probably wouldn't have thought of otherwise. It's difficult to hear someone disagree with you, but try changing your perspective toward those who are opposing you. Don't look at their thoughts and opinions as challenges, but rather as a perspective you have not thought of before. When their words offer you the ability to have a well-rounded perspective on your decision, they give you a gift. In listening to their "why not," you either gain wisdom to help you avoid a bad decision, or you gain additional strength in your decision with a much more effective fallback plan, or your decisions become much more thorough in the process.

You might listen to your naysayers with open ears and think to yourself, "Oh, I hadn't thought of that angle before." Or, "If that were to happen, I'd do this or that." Hopefully this is making as much sense to you as it did for me when I learned about this technique. Will this always stop you from making a bad decision? No, but it will certainly help to minimize them.

Truth cannot be found in feelings, and it can't be established between friends who want to support you just for the sake of supporting you. No, truth has already been decided and written down for our reading pleasure, should we decide to take a moment and read God's word. This is where we will find pure truth. This is where we will find answers to so many questions if we allow them to penetrate our heart and mind. Be as the Bereans: search the scriptures daily. When you make decisions by looking into all the perspectives, your path will stay a little brighter. When your questions are given to God first, and you rest in faith that He will lead you to the path He wants for you, your life becomes more peaceful.

What we all struggle with is that God's way is not ours. His thoughts (and thought processes) are not ours. We do not by nature think like Him, but we CAN. With time and practice, we absolutely can begin to develop the mind of Christ. God wants us to have the same mind, the same thought process, as Christ:

*Have this mind among yourselves, which is yours in Christ Jesus.*

Phil. 2:5

I'd like to recap just a bit before we move to the next chapter. Up until now, we have lived our lives naked and vulnerable to the attacks of the adversary. Unless we spend our time "with intent," fully armored, we leave ourselves unprotected. We are exposed to Satan's schemes, his tactics to undermine the Lord, and he uses you and those around you as the tools to make it happen. Misery loves company, and since he has chosen a path that leads to death, he wants to take down as many as he can while he still has time. Make no mistake—he is coming after you, on a mission of destruction.

Just as a soldier entering the Army needs to be trained in fighting and understanding the enemy, so do we as spiritual warriors need to know who we are fighting. We need to understand the enemy's schemes and covert tactics to take us as prisoners of war. Actual soldiers do reconnaissance work to see what the enemy is up to, and so must we as spiritual warriors.

Our enemy is Satan, the adversary. His schemes and tactics are to make every detour off God's path as attractive and desirable as possible. Our enemy has done his reconnaissance work; he knows our weaknesses, and he will use them to his advantage to get us to move toward him and the path that literally destroys our lives. His tools, his weapons of choice, are lies. Oh, how skillful he is at creating the most enticing lie or the most horrid accusations! Unless we are fully armored, we are left defenseless, ensnared, and bound with chains to the strongholds that keep us from advancing toward the Kingdom—the goal of every child of God.

Are you ready to armor up? Are you ready to put on the full Armor of God? Are you sick and tired of being sick and tired? I know I was. There are enough stories in the Bible to show me that I can rise above my fears, I can reject the lies I have believed, and I can seek truth instead. Instead of being a prisoner of war, in a conflict I never realized I was even fighting, I can be a mighty warrior, a spiritual warrior ready for battle.

My truth is God's truth. I am magnificently made. I am made in the image of God. My physical body is nothing more than a shell that houses who I really am. Whether I have ten toes or none, it does not limit my power and ability as a spiritual warrior. Whether I can say my Rs or even speak at all, my Lord understands me perfectly.

The battles I fight are spiritual, and they include thoughts. The adversary wants to alter truth into a lie to bring me captive—and he can do that initially in my thoughts. He wants to alter my "B" (B.E.A.R.). He wants me to believe a lie, and to fight against my Creator. Just as he tempted Jesus to try and get Him to worship him, the adversary is trying the same thing with me, and with you.

He wants to alter our "E": He wants to capture our emotions, to get us to become angry, to withdraw, to become fearful. He wants to alter our "A": He wants us to act badly—to lash out, point fingers, and blame everything and everyone for why our lives are not abundant. He wants us to follow his methods of making ourselves feel better.

Satan wants us angry, hostile, and resentful. He wants us left wanting—craving physical pleasures, things that we can't afford but we believe we deserve. He wants us to feel lacking in our marriages, so we go after someone else to fill the void. He wants us so stricken emotionally that we will do just about anything to deaden the pain, to quiet the words and voices in our heads that condemn us and tell us we just don't measure up.

When we step back far enough to have clarity, the adversary comes into focus. His schemes and deceptive ways are exposed. "I" am not the adversary's enemy, just as those around me are not my enemy. Satan's fight is with God—we are just his tools. You and I are the weapons he is using. The devil cannot win, but he is on a mission to take down as many as he can while he still has time left.

Our fight is with the adversary, yet we cannot fight a spiritual battle with physical weapons. This has been our downfall. This has been the failure of many people in our lives who have given up the fight—because they fought a physical battle against a spiritual enemy. Our loved ones and friends are soldiers held captive. I have been there, and maybe you have, too: captive to alcohol, drugs, porn, hatred, low self-worth, depression, anxiety/fear, and the list goes on and on. The saddest part of all is that not all prisoners of war "live" to tell their story. Many died in a battle they were not equipped and skilled enough to fight. They died in overdose, suicide, or sickness from something that could have been prevented if they had been fully armored. They were naked warriors.

You can't choose to *not* fight. Your only choice is what side of the battlefield you are going to stand on. The war is continuous, relentless. That's part of Satan's strategy: if he can wear you down, he will get you to give in, give up, surrender.

I choose to armor up. I choose to be fully dressed in the Armor of God. I choose to pick up my spiritual weapon and become as skilled as I can in using it.

You too can be a spiritual warrior. You can be prepared. A spiritual battle means the training and maneuvers are spiritual, yet they result in abundance in your physical life. Abundance is freedom from captivity.

You now know the real enemy you are fighting. It's time to become armed and dressed for War. Are you ready to learn to wear the Armor of God?

# 4

## DRESSED FOR WAR

*Therefore, take up the whole armor of God, that you may be able to withstand in the evil day, and having done all, to stand firm.*

*Eph. 6:13*

In high school in the late '70s, I took some drafting classes and learned I really liked using triangles and compasses to create a drawing complete with dimensions and notes. I loved the idea of taking something I drew and seeing it come to life, for example, as an actual piece of a car. I had been a pencil sketcher as a teenager, mostly drawing portraits. But using dimension was different—way different. It felt more empowering. Instead of sketching something I saw, something I was just replicating, I had the ability to actually "create." After high school, I took some drafting trade classes to get better at this skill.

I remember how scared I was when I applied for a job as a detailer in the early '80s. I had gone through training in high school and advanced training in two trade schools, but still, I wasn't sure I knew enough to be a good detailer. Training was one thing, but doing the real thing was completely different.

I interviewed well and got the job. I quickly learned that the skills I had honed during training hadn't fully prepared me for some of the specifics at my job. I didn't want to ask anyone for help, because I didn't want my co-workers to think I was dumb. Have you ever thought that? Have you ever believed the lie that whispered, "If you don't know something, don't ask"? It's ridiculous. If you don't know something, you don't know it, and truth always simmers to the surface.

Someone who had been in the business for a long time gave me some great advice. He told me, "Make friends with a checker—he will take you under his wing and help you." I used his advice and went to a checker to ask about something I was struggling with. That made all the difference in my drafting career! My career is still going strong, although I've moved beyond a detailer and designer, and have been a Design Supervisor for years. The difference? Seeking guidance from someone more skilled than I.

The same is true when you begin your journey as a spiritual warrior. All the training in the world will not fully prepare you for the variety of battles you will fight. Your success will depend on to whom you choose to listen and keep by your side.

Just as I went to someone who was skilled in a subject I was just learning, I also needed to seek guidance from someone who displayed the spiritual warrior skills I lacked. As a young girl, I went to my mom. I remember one of the most profound things she said to me one day when I came to her for advice, distraught over a boy issue. At the time, everyone around me had a boyfriend. I didn't have one, but in the group of people I hung with, there was one guy who also didn't have a partner. So, we sort of ended up with each other, more out of convenience than because we actually picked each other. Anyway, it seemed like everyone was becoming intimate with each other, and that was something I wasn't prepared for. I didn't like him romantically anyway, so the constant demand for affection became a problem. One night I was given an ultimatum: either we "did it" or we were through.

Wow. I think about that now, and how far I've come—and I would have handled that difficult situation with so much more confidence if I'd been the person I am now. But I lacked self-assurance back then, and certainly didn't have the skills to handle conflict. Ultimately, I didn't give in, so we broke up that day. I remember feeling upset, worrying that I would now be the outsider and not part of the gang. I started to doubt my decision. I came home, dejected, and told my mom the whole story. Remember, I could tell her anything.

Her response has stuck with me to this very day. First, she just listened—she really listened. Then when she started to respond, it wasn't a speech about how I should wait until I'm married to have sex.

She didn't give me all the statistics of STDs or moral or logical reasons for why that kind of behavior would have been bad for me. No, she didn't say any of those things. I told her what he had said—the ultimatum, and the lack of love and respect those words showed. I was pouring out pure emotion to her, and that's exactly how she responded—directly to my heart.

"Aren't you glad you didn't give in to him?" she said. I stopped for a moment to hear her words. They were not at all what I was expecting. I was expecting the lecture, the logic, the statistics. I was even hoping I'd hear them, because any of those would have assured me that my decision to say "no" was a good one.

However, she gave me so much more. She gave me POWER. She gave me VISION. Yes!! I was *very* glad I hadn't given in. In fact, just hearing her words I began to feel the power of self-respect rise within me. I deserved more than that boy's ultimatum, and her words confirmed it! No accusations like, "You shouldn't have gotten yourself into a spot like that," or some other "You should know better" lectures. No, she spoke to my heart, she spoke to my self-respect, and I immediately felt empowered by my decision to say "no."

What if I hadn't gone to my mom? What if I had gone to my friends? Would they have given me sound advice? The emotional war that occurs when we attempt to stand for truth and doing the right thing is very powerful, and the pull to move in the wrong direction, feel bad, or second-guess your decision can be like a magnet.

If I had known that the enemy was Satan and his tool was this boy, and that the weapon Satan was using was the negative thoughts that filled my head, I would have been much stronger to shut him down and not listen to what he was saying. I could have been a much stronger warrior, but I was naked. I was emotionally vulnerable to the adversary, and he immediately threw an arrow of self-doubt at me. The key to the successful outcome of this story was not because I said no out of weakness, but because I sought and received powerful counsel from my mom.

A physical soldier and a spiritual warrior have this in common: they aren't fighting the battle alone! Other soldiers are fighting right alongside them. Not only do you have these warriors (like my mom) standing with you to encourage and comfort you, they are also praying for you. You have the greatest commander in chief, our Heavenly Father, who will never leave you to fight the battle alone, and is always available for instruction and guidance. He is also called the "God of Heaven's Armies," who will call upon His angels to fight for and administer to you in your weakness.

When you're in a spiritual battle, you are never alone. Other spiritual warriors will help you stay strong. It's important you seek counsel from someone who is strong in her faith, will give you wise counsel, speak truth, lift you up, and, of course, will help you dress in the armor of God.

## The Pieces of Armor

> *For you have equipped me with strength for battle; you made those who rise against me sink under me.*

Ps. 18:39

### 1.  The Belt of Truth

We spoke about truth in a previous chapter, but this section is about learning to wrap ourselves in truth in order to *walk* in it. This is the "A" (action)! Knowing how we are created and how our actions follow our beliefs, it's important our paths are set to follow truth and not emotions—or worse, the lies of the adversary.

Truth gives us strength, an inner power that cannot come from the wayward lies of the devil. But how do you get it? How do you know you're walking in truth? Matthew 13 tells us how truth is given: seeds can be planted in any kind of soil (experience), yet the kind of seeds (truth) that actually grow are those in fertile soil. We must be *ready* for the truth. We must have ears to hear. You're reading this—that says you're ready!

The war starts in the mind, in your thoughts. Paul tells us:

> *We destroy arguments and every lofty opinion raised against the knowledge of God, and take every thought captive to obey Christ.*

> 2 Cor. 10:5

There's a lot in this passage. Why would he say that? The thoughts he wants us to capture are those that are contrary to God—thoughts that lean toward our own will instead of God's, and those that are planted by the devil. We are to cast down imaginations. Do you ever overthink things? I do. I can have daydreams of "what if" thinking if I allow myself. Those don't tend to serve me well, and if I give any life to those thoughts, I can become derailed from the right path.

God is not an accuser; he's not itching to punish us as soon as we fall out of line. He is kind and loving. He builds us up when we fall, and cheers for us when we do the right thing. He doesn't give us the negativity the adversary does when he reprimands us. "Go, and sin no more," is how he corrects us. God doesn't start lecturing or condemning us for making wrong choices. So, when you begin to hear this kind of negativity, know it is not God's voice to you.

To gird our loins with truth is about "*walking* in truth." It's not enough to hear or read truth. We must put it into action by walking in it. The two greatest stumbling blocks hindering us from walking in truth are fear and change. Fear is the mother of all roadblocks, and again, not something from God. This scripture is one of my favorites:

> *For God gave us a spirit not of fear but of power and love and self-control.*

2 Tim. 1:7

YES, this is how we were made! We were made with a spirit of power and self-control. We were made to be a spiritual warrior, with the ability to control our feelings and overcome our weaknesses! Everything we need to be successful is already in us! We need to summon these powers if we are to change our basic human nature that instinctively fights against God.

Fear is at the root of anxiety and panic attacks. Fear inhibits us from having clear vision; fear stops us from thinking logically to assess what is truth and what is a lie. Fear can cripple and rob us from having an abundant life.

If you experience anxiety, then you know on a very intimate level the chains that weigh you down when anxiety or panic attacks strike. They seem to come out of nowhere, and then as quickly as they come, they also seem to just disappear. But notice *how* they usually disappear. They usually disappear when you have allowed your feet to follow those thoughts. Let me explain.

Anxiety is the fear that something might happen. When we have anxiety, those fears can overwhelm us and move us in the opposite direction of healing. Anxiety moves us away from what we are afraid of. Those thoughts stop you from going to the party, or being in crowds such as a hockey game or a restaurant.

Anxiety stops us from having an abundant life because the adversary does not want you to have one. In those moments of anxiety, he is imposing his will on you, and you are walking in it. When your loins are girded with fear, your emotions and actions follow, usually by retreating and avoiding. Once you have made the decision to avoid whatever it is you fear, suddenly the fearful emotions and thoughts dissipate, and you feel better.

The cycle continues, and you begin to believe that the way to feel better is to avoid, instead of persevering in truth and strength and facing your fear. Instead of showing up for the battle, you retreat. When we retreat, whether in a physical battle or a spiritual one, the enemy gains ground; the enemy moves closer.

A year ago, while I was up at my cabin in the Manistee National Forest, I was fishing on the dock at the end of my road. There was a young girl, maybe 12 or 13, who was also fishing on the dock. She liked to fish, but she was afraid of *catching* fish, a fear she experienced quite often because she caught a lot of fish. Her fishing was hindered because she couldn't fish without someone who would release her catch for her. I tried to help her not be afraid, but she wasn't ready. She did not have fertile ground for the seeds I wanted to sow; she did not have ears to hear.

Just recently, I was back up at my place of relaxation in the woods. The girl was there again, but this time, she wanted my help. This time she was ready to face her fears and end her anxiety. It's amazing just how fast our life's burdens diminish when we have a mind shift, when we start with the "B" and believe we can do something. It started slow as we took turns catching bluegill. She stood around me and watched as I gave her explicit instructions for taking the fish off the hook.

Then she said, "They have pokey fins." I responded, "Yes, they do, and when you run your hand down those fins from front to back, your hand lays them down and you are too powerful for the fish to stand its fins back up." She timidly touched its side, then its face, then ran her fingers down the side to its tail.

She got braver with each fish we caught. I would hold the fish and she would work at removing the hook. Then we swapped positions; she finally held the fish and I worked out the hook. Eventually, she was holding the fish and taking the hook out. This process didn't take long at all, maybe an hour.

She began asking anyone on the dock if she could take the fish off their hooks. Her fish anxiety was gone.

B.E.A.R.: She just lived it, and the experience was powerful for her. She BELIEVED she was going to touch the fish, and this gave her EMOTIONS of excitement and desire. She put that into ACTION, doing everything I asked her to do. She did it afraid, but she did it. Over and over we caught fish (mostly her), and each time it became easier. The RESULTS? Freedom!

She now had the freedom to fish whenever she wanted, without needing someone to remove the fish. Empowerment! She was empowered to embrace any other fear she had, because she had a real experience that showed when you face your fear, you can overcome! It all starts with the "B," and to have an abundant life, your B must be founded on truth.

The truth is, your adversary *wants* you to fail. He *needs* you to fail. Misery loves company, and he wants to keep company with you. Not because he cares about you, but because he cannot win the war.

Jesus has won the war by overcoming death. We will too, but we must "endure until the end." How do you do that? By understanding truth and then walking in it. The adversary wants to you stumble, to fall, to give up. He does not want you to have the abundant life God promised you.

There is also a peace that surpasses understanding—God's peace. There is nothing greater on this earth. His peace allows the truth to become even clearer, and clear truth increases faith, which allows us to make wiser decisions.

These decisions, based on God's truth, are the foundation of an abundant life. Is your life abundant? I'm not talking about material processions. I'm talking about inner peace within yourself—confidence that whatever you put your mind to do, you will do well. I'm talking about creating an awesome relationship with your Creator who knows the desires of your heart and who is ready to give you good things.

Little by little, truth-transformation begins to happen, and you'll begin to want more and more. You'll want more truth because you will begin to see its powerful impact. You'll start to have confidence, feel emotionally stronger and, of course, be more skilled at seeing the enemy's schemes and tricks.

2.   The Breastplate of Righteousness

> *For the grace of God has appeared, bringing salvation for all people, training us to renounce ungodliness and worldly passions, and to live self-controlled, upright and godly lives in the present age.*

Titus 2:11-12

What is Righteousness? I always think of Abraham. Abraham lived my B.E.A.R. principles. He was a walking example of what it means. Abraham's unwavering belief in God's word and promises was credited to him as righteousness. (Romans 4:20-22)

Abraham's B (Belief) was rock solid, and his E (Emotion) responded to those beliefs by giving all the glory to God. Consequently, his faith was strengthened. He put his beliefs into A (Actions), and the R (Results) of his life were indeed abundant. His B.E.A.R. story is still being talked about thousands of years after his death, and his example of living righteously also lives in the hearts of all who have dedicated their lives to the Lord.

What does the breastplate cover? It covers your vital organs, specifically your heart. When you think of your heart, maybe you think of love, kindness, or gentleness. Our heart is the "E." Our heart is the emotional piece that can drive us into the "A."

Although I'm dissecting each of the B.E.A.R. aspects and relating them to the Armor of God, there is a thread running through each of them that doesn't allow any single piece to work independently. Every piece is woven together and cannot be separated as a stand-alone entity. This is synergy: when the whole is greater than the sum of its parts. When one piece is out of balance, it forces all the pieces to work in an unbalanced manner. We cannot trust our hearts. As much as we may believe we have good intentions, that we are loving, that we know best—we aren't, and we don't. This is hard to accept. God tells us,

*The heart is deceitful above all things, and desperately sick—who can understand it?*

Jer. 17:9

What? No, not mine!

I believed this lie for a long time. I believed I had goodness in me, and that I was a good person. That is, until someone attacks me emotionally, or tells me what my intentions are, as if they can possibly know what is on my mind or in my heart. No, the *real* me comes out when I get backed into a corner. I come out fighting, and it's not pretty. I'm still that scrappy kid from high school, and I can't be bullied. I don't come out of that corner looking good at all! If I am unshielded without armor, I am attacking back, using all the physical weapons I can muster to fight this spiritual battle, and I lose. Every time.

Even if I believe I've won the battle (because I've landed the bigger sting), I've still lost the war. Through my intemperate response, I've damaged relationships—some beyond repair. When I attack in self-defense like that, I've crossed over to the other side—the side of the enemy.

Righteousness is about making Godly choices. Change doesn't happen overnight, although it could; nothing is too big for God. But usually change takes time, and changing our hearts—or at least learning not to rely on what's inside as truth—takes time. It takes living with intent. Every piece of change, every piece of armor we begin to wear, must be done with "intent."

While I know that innately I am not a good person, I've got some additional information to add to that. I alone do not possess goodness, but Christ who is in me does. The good that I do is through the light of Christ, not my own. Our goodness is directly linked to Christ. Jesus tells us,

> *I am the vine; you are the branches. Whoever abides in me and I in him, he it is that bears much fruit, for apart from me you can do nothing.*

> John 15:5

That's a hard saying for some. It was a hard saying for me, too, years ago. "What do you mean? If I don't have God, I don't have anything? Really?" It seems like another life ago that I asked those questions, but I still remember trying to come to terms with "who" I was. The fight for my own personal will was real. I felt that if I gave up my will, that I would lose "me." Instead, I realized when I surrendered my will (for the Lord's), he gave me a greater "me" through *Him*!

I get it now—the whole sum of who I am is greater than the "me" part. The sum of who I am contains Christ in me. That truth makes all the difference. That truth brings humility and a sense of being grounded and balanced. Understanding that truth puts God at the pinnacle of your life, at the core of everything you do, and provides healing waters to your soul.

My Creator is living in me. I'm a host for the Most High! There is not a shred of weakness in that statement. No wonder the adversary wants to knock us off track! Can you imagine what this world would look like if every one of us desired the will of God, and if we had full control of our emotions and desires?

I've had many clients come to me who have endured unbelievable emotional abuse. Their stories are heartwrenching. Sadly, many have allowed the storms of their life to define them. Who they believe they are is exactly where the adversary wants them to "stay." If only they could turn from where they have been and see what magnificent things are ahead of them.

I truly believe the adversary launches his worst attacks on the ones who are the greatest threat to him! Each one of us has a special gift from the Lord. He has blessed each of us with a spiritual gift designed to affect the world in some significant way. Some of us are closer to reaching our potential, and I believe Satan attacks them the hardest. If you feel you're one of those, then perhaps Satan is truly trying to divert you from the righteous path you're on.

I have a little figurine in my office of the Armor of God, a warrior with all the pieces of God's battle gear. Piece by piece I work through the armor with my clients, and we begin to discover the value of wearing it. Every day we must think about God's Armor and decide to wear it with real intent. It's not a natural thing to do. You can't hope you won't need it, because you will.

No, we need to wear it every day, moment by moment. It isn't heavy or burdensome, but the protection is powerful. God would not give us defective armor. God wants us to have a heart for Him. Many people actually begin to lose faith in God and his promises when bad things happen to them. Maybe you're even one of those.

Who wants you to think like that? Yep, it's not God. As much as you may think you've got all the reasons in the world to be angry with God because he didn't answer your prayers, or he didn't protect you (or your loved one), or he just didn't seem like he was there for you—he was. That's an even harder thing to hear. But stay with me for a little bit longer.

God is love. He will never tempt you; He is not your accuser. He wants you to have life, and to have it more abundantly. These things may seem to be in conflict with the current situation in your life. If so, you are experiencing a trial, but we are not defined by the trials that come upon us—we are defined by how we handle them.

The quotes I used earlier comes to mind here: We need to "rock the boat" and "make waves" if we want to become a skilled sailor. We can get book smarts, whether it's a textbook or the Bible, but the real test is out on the battlefield, in the trenches. It is in these trials that we build character.

The great coach John Wooden once said, "Character is what you do when you think no one is watching you." Wearing the breastplate of righteousness means you're obedient to God. It's something you do from the inside out, when you think no one is watching you. It's a genuine offer to God. Character choices make you reflect deep inside yourself. It's not a comfortable place to go at first, but when you know truth is what you need to walk in, you have to look at your heart and purge anything that is not truth and is not of God, and then willingly make the choice to obey Him. This is one of the hardest pieces of armor to wear.

3. The Shield of Faith

*Our soul waits for the Lord; He is our help and our shield.*

Ps. 33:20

A shield is designed to deflect and protect. The only shields I've ever seen in real life are the ones police carry during riots. The design may have changed, and the material may be lighter than the shields people carried in Jesus' time, but the principle and purpose is the same: to deflect and protect.

Everything our adversary does is the opposite of how God intended. Even when the adversary comes cloaked in sheep's clothing, even when everything seems to look right and good, the consequences of following him do not give us an abundant life. We are not protected, and we for sure have not deflected his arrows.

We are fallible; we often make mistakes. We can use these errors as great lessons to develop our character, but our adversary whispers that our mistakes define us. We learn to deflect and protect, but that is completely backwards! When we've made a wrong choice, or we've hurt someone in an argument, or any other behavior that is anything but God-like, we deflect ownership. We become like Adam and Eve and begin finger-pointing and blaming. Instead of owning our portion of any conflict, we protect our pride and self-image and deflect the power to heal. Instead of using God's shield to deflect Satan's fiery arrows, we throw them at others. Instead of using the shield to protect us from the enemy, we use it as a barrier to protect ourselves from the very people we say we love.

According to many of the scriptures that define the use of the shield, we are to stand shoulder to shoulder with others who are carrying their shield.

*Prepare buckler and shield, and advance for battle!*

Jer. 46:3

Shields should be line to line, making a great wall. The power of many! But who do you know who is carrying a shield? Who can you stand with, shoulder to shoulder, and prepare for battle?

Many of us think we have no resources to draw from, yet we do.

*He stores up sound wisdom for the upright; He is a shield to those who walk in integrity.*

Prov. 2:7

*But You, O Lord, are a shield about me, my glory, and the lifter of my head.*

Ps. 3:3

Even if you don't currently know of a spiritual warrior, you have God, and you have all of Heaven's armies. You are not alone. He is preparing you for battle, guiding you into all truth. God is your shield. He is making a way and a path for you to follow, protecting you as you lean on Him, and then He gives you a weapon to defend yourself.

4.   The Sword of the Word of God

*For the word of God is living and active, sharper than any two-edged sword, piercing to the division of soul and of spirit, of joints and of marrow, and discerning the thoughts and intentions of the heart.*

Heb. 4:12

The word of God is our sword and our truth. How many people do you know who are truly open to truth? Especially when the truth demands change. Remember earlier when I said God is love? He is, but he also loves truth. God tells us truth is a double-edged sword. Why?

His word says Jesus did not come to this earth to bring peace; He came to bring a sword. Those aren't my words; they are His in Matthew 10:34. The analogy of the sword as his word is genius.

We cannot be divided in our walk and our belief. Remember, we walk in whatever we believe. God wants you to walk in truth, and he uses his word, the scriptures in the Bible, to teach you truth. Without truth, you will believe every lie. And how would you know a lie if you heard one, unless you know the truth? Can you see how easily we can shift from truth to lie if we are not grounded in truth?

Go back to the story of Jesus when he had just finished his 40-day fast. He was weak on every level imaginable. I know how hungry I get by 10:00

a.m. every day if I haven't eaten, and I know how my positive attitude diminishes over time with each growl in my tummy.

At the weakest moment of Jesus' life, Satan comes to attack. This is when he will attack you, too. He will attack when you are most vulnerable, at the very moment he believes he can be most successful at getting you to believe his lies and follow him. Jesus was at his lowest point when Satan began to bargain with Him. Satan went after hunger, then His faith, and then fame and riches that required a compromise of beliefs.

How did Jesus respond? He took his position. He stood firm out on the battlefield. He drew his sword, the word of God. He began to use it by speaking truth against Satan's lies.

If you want power over a lie, you must know the truth. As you can see, each piece of the armor is unique, but intrinsically connected to all the other pieces. In fact, it becomes difficult to see where one piece of armor stops and the other begins. Can you see the power of truth? Your armor is truth.

Truth allows you to make Godly choices, even when they aren't easy to make. Truth is in the word of God. We must know His word in order to recognize a lie. Wearing the sword is reading and understanding the scriptures, the word of God. And when you know truth, you start to become a skillful swordsman.

Unfortunately, when walking in truth requires you to change, it's natural to recoil. We start on a mission to either justify what we're doing or find someone who will tell us what we want to hear. God calls that having "itching ears."

Whether we are talking about hearing truth in church or out in the world, human nature struggles with truth. The struggle is compounded when it requires change.

When I hear people talk about God and define who He is with such conviction, yet what they speak is completely contrary to what the scriptures actually say, I find myself wanting to pull out my sword and set the record straight. Most of the time the people aren't talking to me, so I just listen. But when such misguided people are speaking directly to me, I find the warrior stance is triggered. Now, you can't see it because it's internal, but the warrior is stirred. I'll be honest—I'm not very skilled with the sword. I know there is a way to use it in a much more gracious way than I do, but I'm still a warrior in training.

There's a delicate way of speaking truth when the person you're talking to truly is ignorant, not malicious. I can't say I have a method or a system, because I don't. I don't get it right more than I care to admit. I do try to focus on the relationship first. If they don't have ears to hear, then you're just "casting your pearls amongst swine," as the scripture says. I'm speaking about this here because it's natural to want to speak about something that excites you. As you begin your warrior journey, you *will* become excited; you will see things more clearly, and you will begin to find that inner peace you've been looking for in all the wrong places.

The sword is truth, but it's a double-edged sword. Why would God describe it that way? A literal double-edged sword is sharp on both sides. It has twice the cutting power as a single-edge sword.

The word of God (the sword) is so powerful it divides things at their very core. "Soul and spirit" can seem almost identical, so close that many would not be able to dissect their differences. "Joints and marrow" are bound together almost inseparably. But the word of God is like a razor-sharp sword that can cut them apart; it is so sharp and piercing that it can discern our thoughts and intents. An unskilled swordsman with a double-edged sword is more likely to hurt himself than if he were using a single-edged sword. A double-edged sword needs a skilled swordsman to use it effectively, and this also goes for a skilled "spiritual warrior" who takes up his sword. Beware of picking up your sword to speak truth, if you yourself are not walking in it. You just might be cut with your own truth.

You are almost fully armored. You have your feet firmly planted; no longer are you looking back at every single mistake you have made, nor are you attaching additional lies of being worthless and a failure. You are designed to be a mighty spiritual warrior, and the enemy has attempted to steal your identity. But no longer. You are on to him, you are learning his schemes and tricks, and you are beginning to speak truth. You have God and His Heaven's Armies to stand shoulder to shoulder with as you raise your shield. You will begin to surround yourself with others who also have the truth. They will be your comrades in the trenches of spiritual wars that will come upon you if you're not already knee-deep into them. You have put on your breastplate of righteousness, which is to surrender your will and walk according to the promises and instructions of the Lord, unwavering in your decisions to do so.

You have a double-edged sword. You may not be very skilled at the moment, but soon you will be. You have one thing left unprotected from the adversary: your head. I have saved the best piece for last.

5.  The Helmet of Salvation

> *Oh LORD, my Lord, the strength of my salvation, you have covered my head in the day of battle.*

Ps. 140:7

I have saved the Helmet of Salvation until last because it's the last piece of armor a soldier or warrior puts on, and yet it covers and protects the part of our body that makes all the decisions. It protects the brain from being injured. Without the ability to make wise choices, we fall victim to the enemy.

Before we step out on the battlefield, we need to be fully armored and prepared for battle. When we are unprepared, no armor or helmet will protect us. However, when we become skilled, we can begin to strategically place ourselves in the best position for success.

What part of B.E.A.R. is the helmet? Remember, the helmet protects the brain, the central intelligence: Belief. Everything starts with the B, because this is the piece we fully control. Whatever you believe, your emotions, actions, and results will follow—and that's true whether you believe the truth or a lie. B→ E. A. R. We always have the ability to look at the R (results), and see if we're on track with an abundant life. That's our promise from God. He doesn't lie. His word is truth.

Take up your helmet and put it on your head. Adjust it until it's in the best position, and then secure the strap. What does this mean? What beliefs do you want? Truth or Lies? (You'll walk in whatever you choose.) How do you get truth? Just as a successful soldier has a skilled physical commander in chief in a war, spiritual warriors also have a commander in chief in all spiritual battles: Almighty God, the God of Angel Armies. Whether it's a physical or spiritual war, you must surrender your will to that of the commander in chief. The helmet helps to drown out the noise and chatter around you so you can fully concentrate on the voice of your commander.

Human nature is designed to fight against God, remember? Without Him, you cannot surrender, you cannot wear the armor, you cannot win the spiritual war. God tells us that without Christ, we can do nothing. Of course, our natural self doesn't want to believe that. It's human nature to believe we are independent, intelligent, and can solve our problems on our own—but can we? We cannot win any wars—spiritual or physical—when we are fighting against God. Remember who the real enemy is, and keep God on your side to fight him.

Take a look at the world around us. Is the crime increasing? Are senseless murders on the rise? Is there really equality? Are marriages falling apart? Are children becoming more disrespectful to their parents and to people in general? We might want to say to ourselves, "Well, *those* people aren't living correctly," but I dare say none of us are!

You have to take a close look at yourself, because you are the only thing you can change in this world, in your home or office, in your marriage, or in your family. None of what you fight is the real enemy. You want to believe it is, because you know exactly who hurt you! Or do you?

While it is true you may have some serious battle scars, both physical and emotional, from the wars you have fought, you truly haven't won anything. When your mind and heart are filled with fear, hatred, resentment, bitterness, anxiety, depression, low self-worth, guilt, or shame, you have surrendered to the enemy.

Remember, the battle is spiritual. To fight it, you have to stand firm against the enemy. The people you struggle to forgive are physical beings—they are not the battles you're fighting, even though you're exhausted from the relentless arguing. It's not your parents, children, spouse, or ex. It isn't the murderer, rapist, or pedophile. It isn't the thief, the drunk-ard, the cancer, or illness.

While you grieve for losses both small and great, none of these are the enemy. The enemy has cloaked himself so cunningly that you are blind-ed to see him—instead, you focus on his *effects*. Thus, you begin to fight against everything *except* the enemy.

All that will change for you now. No longer will you look at the physi-cal struggles in your life and in the world and not recognize the real en-emy. You can only see the results of his lies. God defines spirit very much like wind: you cannot see it or where it goes, but you sure can see its effects. You cannot see Satan or his lies, but you can see how he wrecks people's lives.

As you begin to put your armor on component by component, you be-gin to see that every piece of the armor *is* God. The armor you are putting on "with intent" is God's protective clothing in the form of surrender to His will, Godly choices, and actions that follow your beliefs. That is what following Godly truth means.

Battles can be scary, yet God tells us he did not give us a spirit of fear, but of power. One of the greatest lies our enemy tells us is to not show up for the battle. Sometimes, when you get to the point where you're sick and tired of being sick and tired, you start to muster up the courage to fight back.

This is when Satan goes in for the kill. He hands us lie after lie that sound like "Don't go there. Don't bother. It won't make a difference. You'll just end up losing anyway. You'll just end up getting hurt. It's not worth it. You're not worth it. You deserved it." And on and on he goes with his relentless pursuit of lies—anything to stop you from progressing.

The stage has been set. You are aware of who and what the enemy is. You have learned everything you see is the symptom or tool the devil uses to wage war with you. You also know there is an armor, an internal spiri-tual armor you can put on to protect you from the sting of the devil, from the temptations he puts in front of you to knock you off course.

God has made you a magnificent being with a plan and purpose, and that is why Satan is jealous of your very existence. You have been designed as a powerful spiritual warrior, created to be on an abundant path created specifically for you. You have a spark of God's divinity within you. Let that spark turn into a fire that molds and tempers you! You have been given instructions on how to handle your enemy, including wearing spiritual armor and using spiritual weapons to become victorious.

Your enemy has done everything in his power to deceive you so that you do not follow God. While it is true the battle belongs to the Lord, you must show up for the battle. Showing up is literally half the battle, and it's something you have 100% control over. You can't possibly win a war you never showed up for, right? That's another one of the devil's deceptions: getting you to believe it's better for you to avoid challenges than to stand firm on the battlefield. The adversary hands you the spirit of fear and many accept it without question, and then crumble in midst of the chaos. But now that you are aware of his plan, you will not succumb to his lies.

God did not give you a spirit of fear, but of power. You are going to stand on your battlefield fully armored, surrounded by spiritual warriors including God's angel armies, and you will be victorious.

Now let's find out what it means to stand firm on the battlefield.

# 5

## SHOW UP FOR THE BATTLE

*Put on the whole armor of God, that you may be able to stand against the schemes of the devil.*

*Eph. 6:11*

I hate fighting. Yes, "hate" is a strong word, but if I were to say that I dislike fighting, I don't think that would convey the strength of my displeasure. That isn't to say I don't fight—I absolutely do. I don't do it well, though, and that's because the battles I fight are usually personal attacks, and I can become quite emotionally engaged.

I will stand there completely emotionally vulnerable and go toe to toe with someone, as I slowly begin to sink lower into the dark abyss of anger. Sometimes it feels like anger takes on a life of its own. My defense mechanism moves me off topic, and then I'm all over the place in my verbal war.

Has this ever happened to you? Oh my word, I can't tell you how upset I make myself after the fact. "Why did I even let myself get that upset? It really doesn't matter what they think." Well, it *shouldn't* matter. Everyone is entitled to their opinion, even if I believe their opinion is flawed, right?

I will also fight for things I'm passionate about—like injustice, for example. I will always fight for the weaker one. I think those causes are noble, but these aren't the battles I'm talking about in this chapter.

## Spiritual Battle

How do you show up for a spiritual battle? Where is the battlefield? If we're to armor up and become fully dressed for war, where do we take our positions to stand firm? The more you learn about the Armor of God and how to fully dress for it, the more you become keenly aware of the continuous battle you fight daily.

Every human being has thoughts. As we have discussed previously, thoughts are spiritual, and our mind is the battlefield. So how do you show up for this spiritual battle, if it's inside us? We would not be sent to war in this physical world without first going through boot camp. For an individual to become a soldier, he must be trained. The same holds true for a spiritual warrior.

I have some friends who were in the armed services, so I spent some time with them to discuss their process of moving from a civilian to a trained soldier. Of all the branches of service, I decided to select the Army as my reference point, since there was no Air Force, Navy, or Marines during Biblical times. We know there were many battles on foot and on horses. What I found very interesting, as a friend began discussing his training process, was how much his joining and training for war was so much like our choice to join Christ and train for our spiritual war. My mind is always looking for parallels between earth and heaven, and once again I found another.

Unless there's a draft, those who enlist in the Army do so voluntarily. They join for numerous noble reasons, like defending their country, preserving liberty—or even selfish ones, like escaping from home and finding adventure. What about becoming a Christian? No one is forced to become one. In fact, no one can force you to believe *anything*, even if you go to church regularly. Those who have become true Christians—in their hearts and in their lives—have done so voluntarily.

Now, some people might say they didn't have a choice as a kid; they had to go through spiritual training whether they liked it or not, because their parents wanted them in church or a religious private school. I'm not talking about the forced classes and education. I'm speaking to those who have willfully chosen to lay down their lives and their will to follow Christ. Now we have a parallel.

So what process does a person go through to become a physical warrior? I pick the physical to describe the spiritual because I believe God's word does that as well—just as Jesus did through parables. It's very difficult for us to understand spiritual concepts until we have a tangible physical reference. At least it is for me! To truly understand something, I need a visual aid, and that's what a physical analogy does for me. It's my prop, my help-aid to understand and learn about the spiritual world.

So let's go back to my friend's description about becoming a soldier in the U.S. Army. He enlisted voluntarily in the service. The truth is that he felt it was his last resort—his life wasn't going as he had planned. Many things had taken a turn in the negative direction, starting with losing his father at the age of 14. His coping mechanism was like many of ours, and he attempted to drown the pain in whatever quick-fix opportunities came his way. Nothing was working right for him, and joining the Army, he hoped, would lead to a better life.

He enlisted, but it didn't take long for him to rethink his decision—boot camp and the very hostile drill sergeant worked him over day after day. To drop out, though, would be worse than not enlisting in the first place. He was in it for the long haul.

First there was the basic physical training: lots of drills, exercise, obstacle courses, and repetition. Just at the point where he thought he couldn't do any more, he pushed through just a little further. Every day, he became stronger, faster, and more determined to keep going.

Then there was the mental training: understanding the importance of teamwork, never leaving your partner, and no matter what, doing what the commanding officer told you without question. It was drilled into him. Why was he there? To defend our country—no matter what.

Then there was the training for advanced skills: fighting, using weapons, understanding the enemy, learning the territory of your surroundings. Every aspect of war was carefully thought out and executed in training format, so that when the soldiers found themselves in active combat, they would be ready.

A soldier needs to dress for war: boots, pants, shirt, bulletproof vest, helmet, and, of course, his weapon. Everyone is dressed alike so you can tell the difference between a civilian and a soldier. Every piece of his armor is crafted for the best possible protection from the elements of war or nature.

I'm leaving much of his personal story out, but you get the point: for a soldier to be fit for battle, he must be trained and completely prepared. During this process, many young men and women drop out. They can't handle the pressure, vigorous training, exhaustion, or emotional stress. This training is a "weeding out" process—many are called, but only the strongest emotionally and physically are chosen.

While some people might see this as simply a description of boot camp, I would guess that those of you reading this have seen it as a parable for our spiritual training. Yes, there is a spiritual parallel to this physical story. "Enlisting" is your willingness to follow Christ. Your commander in chief is the Almighty God. Your uniform is the Armor of God, and your weapon is the Sword of the Word of God. Your comrades are those who seek the truth and walk in it, as well as Jesus and the angel armies. The battlefield is your mind, and the enemy is Satan.

I'm only highlighting the Cliff Notes version. The more you begin to see the parallels between physical and spiritual in almost every aspect of your life, the more clearly you will see the true nature of your struggles here on earth.

I've discovered something from reading the stories in the Bible and from talking to people about their Christian conversion: rarely do people turn to God when everything is going great for them.

As we discussed earlier in this book, it's human nature to resist or fight against God, so when things are going great for us, why would we call upon God for help? Now, I don't want the God-fearing people who have everything going for them (wealth, happiness, health, etc.) to be offended by what I'm about to say.

Yes, there are people who have everything going for them who are committed to Christ . . . but think about when their conversion actually started. Did they become converted during a time of ease? Or did the seed get planted in their youth? Did they overcome some trial of poverty or unhappiness so that now they can reflect on their blessings and are grateful?

If you first turned to God in the midst of happiness and wealth, you are very rare indeed.

The scenarios are different for everyone, but God makes reference to those who are very wealthy:

> *It is easier for a camel to go through the eye of a needle than for a rich person to enter the Kingdom of God!*
>
> Matt. 19:24

God gives us this warning because it's so easy to believe we can provide for ourselves when we have money and health. When we have the resources, it's natural to turn to self. God wants us to rest our hope in His promises, not on the treasures of this world.

God calls us all at different stages in our life, and at a point where we are most ready and able to hear him. I'm sure you've heard many stories where a person is at his breaking point, at the end of his rope, unable to break the chains that are binding and hindering him from moving forward in his life—and then when he has nowhere else to go, he turns to Jesus as a last resort. You hear this story far more often than the one where things are going great for someone, when all his needs and wants can be satisfied in an instant, and he turns to the Lord in thanksgiving. Oh, how I wish that were the norm.

I believe God calls us over and over. I don't think it's a one-time shout-out, and you're out of luck if you didn't hear it or were preoccupied with life or misery. No, I think He calls us over and over, and at just the right moment, when we become willing to listen, we are able to hear His still, quiet voice. This can happen whether you're rich or poor.

God tells us to count the cost for following Him. Now, I never heard my soldier friend tell me whether he counted the cost for joining the service, but hearing the details of his story, I'm going to say no, he probably didn't. Why do you think we need to count the cost? Because the road will not be easy, and we need to know if being a Christian is worth the sacrifice to get there.

We need to be able to surrender "everything"—not just money and physical success, but loved ones, parents, children, husband, wife, family, and friends. In order to truly follow God, He must be first in 100% of our lives. When I think about that, I am reminded of Abraham, and how he was willing to sacrifice his precious son Isaac for God. Even as I type this, I get teary.

The love I have for my children is like no other. I'm not sure if the tears are because of the loss I would feel if I were required to make that sacrifice, or because of the fear that I could not make a sacrifice like Abraham's. Thankfully, God doesn't require human sacrifices. However, He does ask you to make spiritual sacrifices many times in your life, when you need to choose who you will follow: God or man.

Trials
Rejoice in a trial? Have you ever done that?

*Count it all joy, my brothers, when you meet trials of various kinds.*

James 1:2

I remember first reading that and thinking how ridiculous that sounded. In the midst of pain, suffering, loss, heartache, or financial struggles, and countless other trials, we are supposed to experience joy? I, for one, should be ecstatic, then! How about you?

This reminds me of a story. Not a tragic one, but it fits here perfectly. A few years ago, we had a big sleepover party with our adult children and a friend who was staying with us during an internship at the University of Michigan. The friend was staying in our basement, a beautiful place to entertain and to host guests.

In the middle of the night, it began to rain. Then it rained even harder. Not too long after the rain started coming down in buckets, our guest awakened my husband and me—holding up water-soaked socks! She had stepped out of bed and sunk into rain-soaked carpet. We did the fastest furniture move in history!

The next day the water had receded, but the carpet and padding were still soaked. I didn't want the wet carpet to stink, so room by room we began peeling up the carpet and padding. During this back-breaking process, our focus was not on the carpet and padding, or on the drywall that would need to be replaced, or all the rehab work our basement would need. It wasn't even on the plumbing bill we'd soon receive. No, our focus was on all the help we had to clean up, and on our gratitude that the only things we lost were a few paperback books.

No matter what happens in your life, you have the ability to decide how you will react and what you will focus on. A flooded basement could have been an awful experience, but I was so thankful for all the people staying at our house that night who were able to move everything either upstairs or off the floor in record timing. As we were moving furniture and cleaning up, I told everyone how thankful I was for their help. I shared with them my beliefs about trials, and how the Lord tells us we should rejoice in them.

One by one, the helpers made this experience even more positive. The greatest part was when my son Corey starting singing. My daughter Kayla followed him—and they both have amazing voices, so it was beautiful. One by one, everyone started singing along, and soon we truly were rejoicing during this trial! While this isn't a tragic story, and our basement got a new look with different-colored carpet, the lesson we all took away from the experience was to look beyond the struggles for the blessings that accompany the storms in our life.

I've shared several trials I experienced as a child. Back then, I knew nothing about "rejoicing" in a trial, nor do I think I could have comprehended it back then. One of the reasons we struggle with understanding that concept is because it requires an outward focus and perspective, yet in a trial we are very inward-focused and shortsighted.

Trials become the training ground for spiritual warriors. Let me give you a real-life example. If a body builder only focused on the level of difficulty he experienced while working out, or the degree of pain and soreness he felt after a workout, he would have a slim chance of reaching his goal.

However, if he had perspective and could stop focusing on his pain, he would be able to see the change in his body and would understand that soreness today means one day closer to the goal. Once the body builder changes his perspective from internally focusing on the pain and difficulty to externally focusing on the results, he can actually "rejoice" through the pain.

Likewise, you and I can deal with our trials if we turn our focus outward and keep our eyes on our goal. Isn't our most important goal to become like Christ? Any trial will help us become more like Him if we bear it with patience and learn compassion for others.

Now, the body-builder analogy in no way can compare to the emotional heart-wrenching trials many of us endure. But the principle still applies. God can make something good come from anything.

Standing on the Battlefield

In May 2013, I got a call from my sister, Terrie, giving me the awful news that she had been diagnosed with colon cancer. I remember feeling numb as I tried to fight the negative thoughts that came flooding into my mind.

Her cancer was aggressive. She had colon surgery to remove the tumor, and she hoped she could have her colon reconstructed soon and get on with chemo, or whatever other options were available to her. She went home to recuperate.

I started making regular visits to her apartment. She loved Family Feud with Steve Harvey, so she and I would compete to see who could get the number-one answer. She was really good at that game, and it was great to see her laugh.

She wasn't much on having serious conversations, but oh, could she talk! I'm not sure I've met anyone else would could talk as much as Terrie. She never seemed to need to stop and inhale or catch her breath.

Cancer scared her, and it scared me, too. She started talking about God, religion, spirituality, and how she felt about things. She talked about herself—where her life was (or wasn't) heading, and how many mistakes she had made throughout her life. Confiding in me was a huge move on her part.

She started talking seriously with me, and I was more in tuned to her now than I probably had been my whole life. We spent a lot of time talking about Jesus, forgiveness, repentance, and her thoughts about where she might end up (fearing she would go to hell instead of Heaven). Well, there's no time like the present to lay it at the feet of Jesus. As we talked, I could see the spiritual war begin to wage. It was a war she was so familiar with, one she was tired of fighting, and one she almost always wanted to fight on her own.

But we can't fight wars alone. When the adversary's lies have managed to penetrate your mind, it can feel like he or one of his entourage seems to just take up residency. You become consumed with negativity and self-doubt, and the battle inside your mind is a relentless emotional blow over and over and over again. It seems the more you try to fight it, the fiercer the negative self-speak becomes. We all have those negative thoughts that hammer at our self-esteem, but some people are simply more armored than others. Some are more skilled at speaking "truth" to that negativity, and through practice are better sword fighters than others.

The armor creates distance to give you clearer vision, and the sword of the word of God is what we use to fight against that negativity. The greatest thing we *must* do—and this is something so important and powerful that many miss it—is to show up for the battle! What does that mean? While it is true that the battle belongs to the Lord, you can't stay in bed and throw the covers over your head and tell God to let you know how it ends. No, that doesn't work at all. In fact, many aren't even sure why they fight the same battle over and over again, with the same negative ending. It might be because they aren't showing up for the battle.

Remember: STAND FIRM, STAND FIRM, STAND FIRM. Three times God uses that phrase in Ephesians 6:11-14, and I believe when God uses a phrase three times in a short passage, He wants you to pay close attention. We *must* take our position. Think about soldiers—to fight, they must take a stand, they must take their position, and they must assuredly show up on the battlefield.

So after years of my sister being a naked warrior (emotionally and spiritually), and at a time in her life where her emotions were raw, she began to take a stand. She spoke truth in scripture as we studied together. One of the greatest lies Satan tells us is that we're "too far gone," that God could never love us or forgive us. This was a very heavy chain that hung on my sister, but the chain finally broke!

This is the B. This is where Satan wants to take up residency long enough for us to Believe the lie. Remember, once we do, our Emotions respond to it, and our Actions drive us in that path. Are you on a path to negative Results? Are you on a path that doesn't give you an abundant life, or that says you're not good enough, or you're not lovable, or that "Nothing will ever change?" Just like my sister, you too can start packing the bags of the adversary's lies and kick them out with truth!

Ephesians 6 is about taking ACTION. It's this action that makes the difference for every single one of us. You hear stories about how one person experiencing a tragedy can be triumphant in how he handles it, while others experiencing the exact same tragedy seem to crash and burn. It's the B! When we change the B, the EAR comes along for the ride. Isn't that interesting? The EAR . . . yes, what we *listen* to also changes! We listen to TRUTH, and in that truth, it allows us to be triumphant even in the midst of a trial. Can you experience joy in that? Now maybe that is starting to make a little more sense.

My sister received hospice care. The cancer was too aggressive, and she wasn't strong enough to even begin chemotherapy. She studied the scriptures, purged enough lies to see God's truth about who she really was, and then was moved to be baptized. We talked about the figurative expression "dead to the world but alive in Christ," and how that would be literally true for her. I couldn't have been more excited for her. She changed her belief system and her emotions positively responded. She showed up for the battle; she took action and the end result was salvation. Hallelujah!

The greatest trial I have ever experienced in my life was being in that hospice room all alone with my sister as she passed away from colon cancer. It had spread to her lungs and liver. She found out in May she had cancer, and by September she was gone. That night seemed to last forever. But at 6:00 a.m., she took her last breath, and her suffering stopped. At that very moment, I said to myself, "The next thing she will see will be her Savior." In that very moment I recognized my sister had believed Truth. Her emotions had been stirred to take action, and that path resulted in the best decision of her life.

As for me, I had been fearful to lose my sister alone. Everything in my being said to throw the covers over my head and have someone tell me when it's over. But instead I showed up on that battlefield. Against all my fear, all my emotions that attempted to overwhelm me, I stood firm and took my position in that hospice room. As sad as I was to lose my sister, I was at peace with an awesome closure. I was at peace knowing she called upon Jesus and He answered. I will see her again!

You are Not Alone

I realized I was not alone in that hospice room with my sister. I had so many prayer warriors with me. I had her boys there in spirit, and my parents. And most of all, I had Jesus. He was right there, giving me comfort, giving me strength to tell my stories to my sister, and giving me power to sing and praise Him.

Angels were created to help us, remember:

> *Are they not all ministering spirits sent out to serve for the sake of those who are to inherit salvation?*

Heb. 1:14

They help to strengthen us in time of need. The angels administered to Jesus after he had fasted for 40 days and warred with Satan. I believe they administered to me that morning, too.

I was never alone.

When I say we are not alone, that's what I mean *literally*. We tend to look around us, and if we don't see anyone, then we "believe" we are alone. God tells us otherwise.

In fact, there is a great story in the Bible about a prophet named Elisha who was with a young man, and this young man was very much like us, in that he walked by sight and not by faith.

You can find the story in 2 Kings 6:8-23. Israel was at war (again) with Syria. Elisha had a gift of being able to predict where the armies of Syria were, and Elisha would tell the Israelites the strategies of the king of Syria's army. That greatly disturbed Syria's king. He had about enough of that, so he decided to gather together a great number of soldiers with the intent of capturing Elisha.

It was a covert operation, and the armies of Syria moved in and surrounded Elisha during the night. When Elisha woke up, he was surrounded by many soldiers, chariots, and horses. A young man who was with Elisha was scared and asked Elisha what they should do. This young man was walking in the flesh, only focusing on what he could see.

Elisha told him to not be afraid, and told him there were more on their side than on Syria's side. I can image myself looking around at the great number of enemy soldiers, and then looking at the two of us and wondering where Elisha got his math skills. Then Elisha prayed,

> *"O Lord, please open his eyes that he may see."*

> 2 Kings 6:17

The Lord opened the young man's eyes, and when he looked up, he saw that the hillside around Elisha was filled with horses and chariots of fire.

There is more to this story, but the point I want to make is that we need to have faith to believe God's word when He says we are not alone.

In the case of this young man, when his eyes were opened, it was no longer faith—it was fact. God wants us to act on faith. I believe this story shows us that we are truly not alone. Walk by faith, not by sight!

When we shift our focus away from ourselves and outward to what is around us, we will see help, we will see light, we will see hope.

Wars will never cease. Without truth, you will believe and live out Satan's lies. Without the Armor of God, you will be naked, emotionally vulnerable to the attacks of the adversary. Without the Armor of God, you will most assuredly and unknowingly surrender to the enemy.

To recap before we move on:

The wars are relentless; the adversary has lost and wants to take down as many as he can in the process. He is jealous of you and wants you to fail. But you are a mighty warrior! You know your enemy; you are on to his schemes now and his lies have no power when you know the truth. You know the pieces of the armor are spiritual—they are spiritual thoughts put into action. Fully armored, you can quench the fiery arrows of the devil. The Armor of God gives you protection and clarity to understand what is truly happening. You are ready to take your place on the battlefield. You are dressed and ready for war.

# 6

# THE WAR

*You will not need to fight in this battle. Stand firm, hold your position, and see the salvation of the Lord on your behalf. . .*

*2 Chron. 20:17*

War—it's everywhere. The news is filled with stories of violence and killing, terrorist attacks, spousal abuse, bullying, and suicide. I find myself sickened every time I turn on the TV or watch something stream across my phone. In my counseling life, the stories I hear get darker and more heartwrenching. As the Bible predicted, the love of many are waxing cold.

Exactly what or who are you fighting? Your spouse? Your children? The rude person on the highway? Your boss or someone at work who seems to be out to get you? To know exactly what we're fighting, we must go to the source of truth, the Bible:

> *For we do not wrestle against flesh and blood, but against the rulers, against the authorities, against the cosmic powers over this present darkness, against the spiritual forces of evil in the heavenly places.*

*Eph. 6:12*

What does that mean exactly? It means our battle is not physical—it's spiritual. We can't physically see what we're fighting. So, the answer to my question above is, "None of those people." But if the battle is spiritual, how do you fight it? How do we fight something if we can't see it?

I love how God has thought of EVERYTHING! God put us here in this physical world and tells us the battles we fight are spiritual. He also tells us how to fight this kind of battle if we are to be victorious.

So what does He say? How do we fight this type of battle?

> *For though we walk in the flesh, we are not waging war according to the flesh. For the weapons of our warfare are not of the flesh, but have divine power to destroy strongholds.*

> 2 Cor. 10:3-4

What? My weapon is not of the flesh? Oh my, this seems much harder than I first thought it would be. I'm a physical person, and I thought I was fighting physical people. But the Bible tells me "don't war according to the flesh," and my weapons are "not of the flesh," either. I needed more help when I first learned this, and I'm sure you do, too.

This is where the rubber meets the road—where you stand on the battlefield as a warrior, and put everything into play that you've read in this book. The success of our battles depends on having God and his angel armies on our side. We must choose Him.

So many of the battles we read in the Bible focus on kings—many stories outline the rise and fall of kings both good and bad. The success or failure of the battles depended on the kings' relationship with the Lord. Those who followed after the Lord were highly successful. Those who followed after their own will, or followed after other gods, came to nothing and lost the battle.

Where you are in life right now is the result of what you believe. All of us believe lies—maybe not every lie, but enough of them to create struggles in our life. What do you believe? What war do you seem to struggle with? Anxiety? Depression? Self-worth? Abandonment? Relationship issues with family, spouse, parent, or children?

The emotional wars you fight are spiritual in origin, and they are a result of believing the adversary's lies. When we lose a battle, we are scarred and become insecure, fearful, or angry. Failed marriages leave us scarred and insecure. Abusive relationships leave us fearful and believing our lives are worthless. Arguments and fights leave us angry. When these negative experiences are not resolved but are left to fester, they can result in hatred, resentment, and self-loathing.

There is no excuse for anything negative that happened to you. Nothing justifies hurting another human being, whether it's physically, emotionally, or verbally. How do you respond when you've been hurt? Either you lash out, or you internalize it and let it fester within you.

Internalizing it means you believe (the lie) that you deserved it, and you begin to speak negatively to yourself. The choices you make can look very much like your own physical abuse: you start using alcohol, drugs, and maybe you become abusive to others. Your relationships can become abusive, because when you believe you deserve less, you choose less. You don't need the world's punishment—you do it to yourself.

If you lash out at what you believe is the cause of your pain, you can damage or even destroy relationships. If you believe life is unfair, you begin to blame everyone else for your misery, and you start living with resentment.

If you respond by either lashing out or internalizing, you're human—that's just the physical side of you reacting. You are walking in the flesh, not in the spirit. But either response keeps your feet firmly planted right where you are: fighting the same fight. You're just fighting the symptom of believing the enemy's lies, not the enemy himself.

Remember, if you can "see" it, then that is not your enemy. Your enemy isn't physical—this is the hardest part to understand. When you are hurting the most, it is difficult to look at the one who has hurt you with compassion, love, or forgiveness. Remember, human nature fights against God, so in our responses of the flesh, we say hurtful things, we lash out, and we wound others.

We have this unbelievable desire to "get even" or to "mete out justice." With each hurtful event, the more emotionally guarded we become.

This guard, this type of protective shield, is not the Armor of God, but rather the wall of lies we build by believing the adversary. This wall does not mend or fix or bring peace and forgiveness. This wall recoils, rejects, and justifies itself. This wall grows thicker with each sting, and we are left without answers or hope. We are left completely naked.

Life and all its trials may have left you bitter and resentful, even to (maybe especially to) God. It is difficult to follow after God when our hearts are hurting, especially if we believe God has failed us. I hope that reading this book has helped you see that the idea that God has failed you is yet another lie. If the adversary can get you to turn from God—B, the belief in Him—the rest follows automatically. This above all else is Satan's greatest destructive lie: that God has failed you. He most assuredly has not.

When our hearts turn to God, we see real truth, and we have the ability to forgive. Forgiveness heals. We need forgiveness from God, and we need to forgive others. Most importantly, we need to forgive ourselves.

When someone hurts me, forgiveness is the last thing I want to do. In the past, I believed the lie that if I selfishly held back my forgiveness, that I was somehow holding that person hostage. I was attempting to deliver my own judgment and sentence upon them. "They didn't deserve to be forgiven," I would think. "After all, look what they've done." I know I'm not alone in these thoughts—you might have thought that a time or two.

I learned another truth I'd like to share—something that has freed me from so much emotional baggage, and I hope it frees you, too. I learned that forgiveness is something you do for yourself! Now before you think I'm just talking about getting rid of the anger and resentment—which is awesome by itself—it's much more than that.

I believe we will all eventually meet our Maker. When you finally meet Him, what do you think He will say to you? Will He say, "Well done, my faithful servant?" Will he completely forgive you? Will your slate be wiped clean? These might seem like strange questions, but continue reading.

Here is the greatest gift we give ourselves when we forgive:

*For if you forgive others their trespasses, your heavenly Father will also forgive you, but if you do not forgive others their trespasses, neither will your Father forgive your trespasses.*

Matt. 6:14-15

Whoa. That's a bit sobering, maybe even shocking. The quality of forgiveness I receive from my Maker is directly proportional to the forgiveness I give to others! That's quite a different perspective than the lie we believe. Most of us don't want to forgive because the other person doesn't "deserve" it. But *we* want to be forgiven completely. *We* want to deserve it—but then we have to walk in it. It's a spiritual walk because it goes against our human nature! But the truth is, none of us deserve forgiveness. That's why we need God's grace—because none of us merit his blessings.

When we stand before our Maker (whenever that time comes), what do you want Him to remember about your mistakes, your sins, and your past? NOTHING! You want your slate wiped clean. But we play a huge part in that—we must display the same kind of forgiveness we want to feel from our Heavenly Father. Indeed, forgiveness is a gift we give ourselves!

Forgiving those who have hurt you can feel emotionally brutal, but it's the greatest gift you can give yourself. As I stated earlier, the byproduct of forgiveness is the shedding of emotional baggage. But the hardest one to forgive is yourself. The adversary will do everything in his power to keep you looking backwards, to keep you focused on every sin and mistake you have made and then fill your head with lies of unworthiness. But what does God say? Does He want you to stay there or move on?

*Brothers, I do not consider that I have made it my own. But one thing I do: forgetting what lies behind and straining forward to what lies ahead, I press on toward the goal for the prize of the upward call of God in Christ Jesus.*

Phil. 3:13-14

God wants the very best for each and every one of us. He has GREAT plans for us.

> *For I know the plans I have for you, declares the Lord, plans for welfare and not for evil, to give you a future and a hope.*

Jer. 29:11

He has given us hope and vision. We are his greatest creation. We are magnificently made. He designed us to be a mighty powerful spiritual warrior, and he has something so incredible waiting for us. YES, I want the prosperous and abundant life He has promised. And I want something else, something I have thought about my entire life:

> *What no eye has seen, nor ear heard, nor the heart of man imagined, what God has prepared for those who love him.*

I Cor. 2:9

I remember as a young girl, I kept trying to imagine what He had prepared for me. I knew I couldn't ever come up with it, but that didn't stop me from trying. I would think of the most incredible thing and say to myself, "Oh, but it's better than that!" When I got older, I'd still think about it, although my thoughts had matured and changed. Still I would think, "Oh, it's even better!"

God has prepared something so glorious we can't even imagine it, and our experience on Earth can't even begin to compare.

> *For I consider that the sufferings of this present time are not worth comparing with the glory that is to be revealed to us.*

Rom. 8:18

When I was younger, and I felt the fiery sting of the adversary, that last statement bothered me. I had never experienced any kind of hurt where later I could say the pain did not even compare with the joy I was experiencing. That is, until I had a child. That pain for me was unbearable. After 21 hours of labor, seven of which were with Pitocin and Demerol . . . I was only dilated to a four. The pain was excruciating, and I finally ended up with a C-section. In some very small way, I began to understand that scripture in Romans. The pain I experienced in labor did not compare to the joy I had of seeing a beautiful child looking up at me. What God has in store for me is even greater than that! So much greater!

God gives wisdom and discernment to those who ask for it. Are the things we suffer a result of believing a lie? Perhaps they are the result of someone *else* believing the lie. Discernment will help you separate the two; wisdom will move you in the right direction.

Sometimes the suffering is what you do for others. Christ's suffering wasn't about Him at all, but about others. He was an example for us in all things—so are we suffering for a purpose greater than our own?

Faith means believing that the suffering we experience here on Earth has a greater purpose. Much of the time we focus internally on our own suffering. Perhaps our focus needs to be external, just like it was for Jesus. Perhaps there is something else we learn when our focus is not on self.

Training

What makes a Christian warrior different? Notice I didn't say "better!" We have all sinned and fallen short of the glory of God. No one is better than anyone else. However, a Christian warrior needs to be different. One of those distinguishing areas is how we respond to our enemies. God says to love them. When I first read that after an emotional breakup, I thought to myself, "Are you kidding me right now? Did you see what he did to me? Do you see how much I'm hurting?" There was nothing I could have said or done in the flesh that would have taken away my pain. But I thought it would. I remember how torn I was, wanting to lash out, wanting to right the wrong and deliver my own judgment on how I thought the score should be settled. But I didn't. I put on the armor, every single piece. Each piece was put on with intent, securely strapped in place.

I delayed my responses to give me time to hear the soft quiet words of my Lord. Putting on the armor enabled me to distance myself enough to calm my spirit.

I found myself becoming an emotional rollercoaster, and I would inadvertently forget to put my armor on and BAM . . . there I was fully naked again, feeling the sting, feeling the hurt and anger beginning to rise once more. Again, I put the armor back on.

The lesson I learned was that the default position of the armor is always OFF. It can only be put on "with intent!" When I was fully armored, I was calm and I thought with clarity. I didn't own things that were not mine to own, and I could see deep places that needed to change within me. It gave me a different perspective, and yes, I was able to love my enemy.

Standing in the armor prevents you from paying evil with evil. We are to take the higher road, despite what has been said or done to us. God tells us,

> *Do not be overcome by evil, but overcome evil with good.*

> Rom. 12:21

The more you read about how we are supposed to respond to those who have hurt us, the more we can see we need the armor to protect us from the adversary's fiery arrows, to give us distance to see things more clearly, and to allow us time to respond in love.

There is always an internal war, always a struggle to overcome. This battle is flesh versus spirit; walking with human nature responses or with spiritual ones. How should we respond to those who hurt us? In spirit—after the likeness of Christ. Paul tells us,

> *I appeal to you therefore, brethren, by the mercies of God, to present your bodies as a living sacrifice, holy and acceptable to God, which is your spiritual worship. Do not be conformed to this world, but be*

> *transformed by the renewing of your mind, that by testing you may discern what is the will of God, what is good and acceptable and perfect.*
>
> Rom. 12:1-2

Did you catch that? God wants us to renew our mind. That is how we become transformed. It starts with the "B" . . . and the rest follows on autopilot! Up until now, the battle you have fought with the enemy has been merely a symptom of the greater illness: believing his lies.

Now, one of the greatest lies Satan tells us is that if we just "believe" that Jesus was the son of God, then—poof!—we're saved. While the scriptures do say we must *start* by believing, it's only a piece of the puzzle. That is only the B—what about the rest of B.E.A.R.? This acronym is also perfectly weaved into our salvation.

What is the E? The emotions that lead your heart to repentance. It is the surrendering of your heart to God and to His will. It is the recognition that your life has not lined up with the amazing plan God created for you.

What is the A? It is putting away all things in action and thought that are contrary to God. It is giving up your sins to know Him. It is putting off the natural man and becoming like Him. Action moves you to baptism, or if you already have been baptized, to a recommitment to God. Action means to turn away from Satan and his life of lies and chaos and turn to God, toward the magnificent plan he has for you.

And the R? The results are an abundance of joy and blessings, not just in this life, but in the life to come. I spoke earlier of the scripture in I Corinthians, and it bears repeating: no eye has seen, and no mind can comprehend or even imagine what God has in store for those who believe. It's impossible for us fully understand his plan for us.

Faith is believing that God's abundance is beyond our imagination. Faith is what allows us to put every part of B.E.A.R. into motion. The Armor of God is your protection and shield, giving you the ability to walk in God's plan and to clearly hear His truth.

The Battle Isn't Over

Believing truth, of course, does not mean the battle is over. In fact, some of the battle hasn't actually begun yet.

The adversary wants you to stay where you are. He wants to you remain broken, weak, and emotionally naked. He wants to you feel every single arrow he throws. As long as you're vulnerable and defeated, you're no threat to him. However, exposing his schemes and tricks and awakening the mighty warrior inside you sets the stage for another war.

Paul was an expert in this area. Paul persecuted God's people and the church of God. But like you, he too had his eyes opened and was saved. When he changed from killing Christians to preaching about God, the tables turned and Paul was the one being persecuted—by both the Jews and the Gentiles! It will be the same with you. People who know your sins, your mistakes, and your past, will want to bring all those things to memory. But just as with Paul, your past does not define you!

I can't imagine how I would have responded to Paul if I had lived in his day. Probably after the flesh (human nature) and not the spirit (Godly nature). I probably wouldn't have wanted to give him the time of day—I mean, why should I listen to him after he's killed my Christian friends? I'd like to think my faith, beliefs, and spiritual walk is stronger than that now.

In a very small way, I can relate to Paul. I can relate to trying to walk after the spirit instead of the flesh, yet being constantly reminded of the sins of my past. It's not just me bringing them to mind, but others who didn't like this change—or believe that I've truly changed. This is the next war, so I am preparing you for it. There will be those who persecute you for attempting to follow after the spirit. Stay the course!

> You have heard that it was said, "You shall love your neighbor and hate your enemy.  But I say to you, Love your enemies and pray for those who persecute you, so that you may be sons of your Father who is in heaven..."

Matt. 5:43-45

Did you catch that? Did you see the reason why we are to be different? "SO THAT YOU MAY BE SONS OF YOUR FATHER WHO IS IN HEAVEN."

The scripture goes on to talk about making sure we're not showing love only to those who love us:

> *For if you love those who love you, what reward do you have? Do not even the tax collectors do the same? And if you greet only your brothers, what more are you doing than others? Do not even the Gentiles do the same?*

Matt. 5:46-47

We are to respond in love to everyone. God is no respecter of persons, so we shouldn't be, either. Yes, it's a hard walk, but you'll soon discover that the walk demands that your focus is on others instead of yourself. Jesus is outward-focused; Satan is inward-focused. I want to be like Jesus, and I'm sure you do, too.

We can't do it naked. Your life will begin to take on a whole new perspective when you begin to put on the pieces of armor. Real truth is not found in the world, but in the word of God.

When you begin to display the same love as Jesus, who was unwavering in his love for his Father, you will see your life transform. You can begin to be like Abraham, who gave us a great example of faith, who walked after the Spirit and followed the voice of the Lord—not the will of his own heart. Abraham's choice to follow the instruction of God rather than man was counted as righteousness. Abraham wore the breastplate well.

You too can wear the Armor of God well! This isn't a physical shield, it's a spiritual protective covering. It isn't something external you put on, but rather something you internalize. The armor becomes part of you, and if you wear it constantly, you'll find that you and the armor are inseparable—your will and God's will can become one.

Putting on the Armor of God commands a different thought process and belief system. It prompts you to move in ways that don't come naturally when we're thinking with a "carnal" mind. It empowers you and gives you courage to show up for the battle. A fully dressed spiritual warrior allows God to break the chains that imprison you. This is what the scriptures mean by "the Truth will set you free." Everything is in place for you to successfully take your victory crown.

Strike a Victory Pose

A victory pose is not a successful warrior's show of arrogance and pride. Being victorious does not mean being better than others. You can strike a victory pose when you have surrendered your life to Christ, you have put on the full armor of God, you have taken your place on the battlefield, you have stood firm in war, and God has fought your battles for you. Paul tells us,

> *As for you, always be sober-minded, endure suffering, do the work of an evangelist, fulfill your ministry. For I am already being poured out as a drink offering, and the time of my departure has come. I have fought the good fight, I have finished the race, I have kept the faith. Henceforth there is laid up for me the crown of righteousness, which the Lord, the righteous Judge, will award me on that Day, and not only to me but also to all who have loved his appearing.*

2 Tim. 4:5-8

Paul's life wasn't easy, and neither is ours. Remember, character grows in the midst of trials. Consider yourself in the midst of a growth spurt!

Your past does not define you; storms do not define you. But your choice in how to navigate them does define you and shows what you are made of. The right choices lead to a more abundant life. These choices give you the ability to stand firm with confidence in God's promises, and to watch with great expectation as the God of Heaven's armies does the fighting for you.

May you be transformed by the renewing of your mind—may you be fully dressed for war and take your position out on the battlefield. Stand firm, my friend. You are not alone. I am with you in spirit, others are praying for you, and the God of Heaven's armies are doing the fighting for you. Your unwavering faith put into action will be counted as righteousness. Stand firm as you watch God conquer your battles.

> *For everyone who has been born of God overcomes the world. And this is the victory that has overcome the world – our faith.*

1 John 5:4

May you be richly blessed, my fellow Warriors.

If you enjoyed this book, please be so kind and leave a review on Amazon. Here is the Amazon link to this book: http://amzn.to/2fj5iUo

For this and any other books by Kim M. Snyder visit:
http://thepowerinparenting.com/KimMSnyder_Author

# ABOUT THE AUTHOR

Kim Snyder holds a Master's degree in Mental Health Counseling from Walden University. A Licensed Professional Counselor in Michigan, she has a private practice called The Power in Parenting, where she specializes in helping families with parenting-related challenges. Kim's philosophy centers on creating healthy individuals in order to create healthy families. In her practice, she helps adults see that the emotional baggage they carry from their childhood affects the way they parent their own children. She focuses on helping parents and others become confident and empowered leaders in their families and in their lives.

Kim is also an author and public speaker. Through courses, webinars, conferences, and counseling, she has helped thousands of people navigate the challenges and battles they face by becoming spiritual warriors, dressed in the armor of God.

Kim and her husband, Tim, have four children and live in Livonia, Michigan.

# SCRIPTURE ENCOURAGEMENT

*Be not quick in your spirit to become angry, for anger lodges in the heart of fools.*
   Eccles. 7:9

*Trust in the LORD with all your heart, and do not lean on your own understanding. In all your ways acknowledge him, and he will make straight your paths.*
   Prov. 3:5-6

*For I, the LORD your God, hold your right hand; it is I who say to you, "Fear not, I am the one who helps you."*
   Isa. 41:13

*Peace I leave with you; my peace I give to you. Not as the world gives do I give to you. Let not your hearts be troubled, neither let them be afraid.*
   John 14:27

*I have said these things to you, that in me you may have peace. In the world you will have tribulation. But take heart: I have overcome the world.*
   John 16:33

*God is our refuge and strength, a very present help in trouble.*
   Ps. 46:1

*Have nothing to do with foolish, ignorant controversies; you know that they breed quarrels. And the Lord's servant must not be quarrelsome but kind to everyone, able to teach, patiently enduring evil, correcting his opponents with gentleness. ...*
   2 Tim. 2:23-25

*Know this, my beloved brothers: let every person be quick to listen, slow to speak, slow to anger; for the anger of man does not produce the righteousness of God.*
   James 1:19-20

*Casting all your anxieties on him, because he cares for you.*
   1 Pet. 5:7

*Anxiety in a man's heart weighs him down, but a good word makes him glad.*
   Prov. 12:25

*My comfort in my suffering is this: Your promise preserves my life.*
   Ps. 119:50

*It was good for me that I was afflicted, that I might learn your statutes.*
   Ps. 119:71

*In my distress I called to the LORD, and he answered me.*
   Ps. 120:1

*No, in all these things we are more than conquerors through him who loved us.*
   Rom. 8:37

*Blessed is the man who remains steadfast under trial, for when he has stood the test he will receive the crown of life, which God has promised to those who love him.*
   James 1:12

*The one who conquers, I will grant him to sit with me on my throne, as I also conquered and sat down with my Father on his throne.*
   Rev. 3:21